## Praise for *The Winter Harvest Handbook*

"How do you produce first-rate food all year-ro... is the big question facing the local food movem... of America's most innovative farmers, has come ...cellent answers. Brimming with ingenuity, hope, and eminently practical advice, *The Winter Harvest Handbook* is an indispensable contribution."
—MICHAEL POLLAN, author of *The Omnivore's Dilemma* and *In Defense of Food*

"I just finished picking my first carrots, beets, and radishes from my new 'cold house' in Bedford, New York. It is so rewarding to harvest fresh vegetables and salads in the middle of winter and I grow them following the techniques of Eliot Coleman. I have been a devotee of Eliot's for years, fully agreeing with his methods for growing in winter, spring, summer, and fall, tasty, nutritious produce with a minimum consumption of fossil fuels. Congratulations on another volume of useful, practical, sensible, and enlightening information."
—MARTHA STEWART, best-selling author, magazine publisher, and Emmy Award-winning television producer and host

"Eliot Coleman's books have been called Bibles for small farmers and home gardeners. I suspect that's because he writes about not just gardening but about everything that connects to good food and pleasure; a Renaissance man for a new generation, he'll quote Goethe in the same breath as Ghandi, and as a result, you'll dig, weed, eat, think, and live more fully."
—DAN BARBER, Chef, Blue Hill and Blue Hill Stone Barns

"If we are going to create a good, clean, fair food system, we've got to learn how to grow affordable, local food year-round and make a living at it. Eliot Coleman knows more about this than anyone I've met. Here he gives the detailed information needed to make it work. The only way to learn it better would be to follow him around for a few seasons."
—JOSHUA VIERTEL, President, Slow Food USA

"'Attention to detail is the major secret to success in any endeavor,' writes Eliot Coleman in this absorbing and happily detailed report on his ongoing efforts to grow flawless vegetables without hothouses on the frozen 'back side' of the year. In chapters covering everything from The Yearly Schedule and Greenhouse Design to Weed Control and Marketing, Coleman tracks his own constant search for perfection, a quality that has led more than one young farmer to exclaim 'I'd follow him anywhere.' Well worth reading even if you don't grow vegetables, just to watch a master's mind at work."
—JOAN DYE GUSSOW, author of *This Organic Life*

"*The Winter Harvest Handbook* is a treasure trove of practical, proven techniques for producing crops on a year-round basis in any climate. Based on decades of on-farm research, this book is packed with useful ideas, tips and practices that anyone can use in pursuing the increasingly vital dream of local, organic food production using a minimum of precious resources. A masterful book from a master organic farmer. I wish I had had a copy 35 years ago!"

—AMIGO BOB CANTISANO, President, Organic Ag Advisors

"Eliot Coleman is widely recognized as the 'master' of the master gardeners. His new book, *The Winter Harvest Handbook*—which tells us how to produce local food even in winter in cold climates like Maine, without a lot of energy—now joins his other delightful books as another lovely read, packed with powerful and practical ideas that every gardener will treasure."

—FREDERICK KIRSCHENMANN, Distinguished Fellow,
Leopold Center for Sustainable Agriculture, and President
of Stone Barns Center for Food and Agriculture

# *The* Winter Harvest Handbook

Year-Round Vegetable Production
Using Deep-Organic Techniques
and Unheated Greenhouses

## Eliot Coleman

Photographs and Illustrations
by Barbara Damrosch

CHELSEA GREEN PUBLISHING
WHITE RIVER JUNCTION, VERMONT

Project Manager: Emily Foote
Developmental Editor: Fern Bradley
Copy Editor: Cannon Labrie
Proofreader: Helen Walden
Indexer: Lee Lawton
Designer: Peter Holm, Sterling Hill Productions
Photographs and Illustrations: Barbara Damrosch, except where otherwise noted

Printed in the United States of America
First printing March, 2009
10 9 8 7 6 5 4 3    09 10 11 12 13 14

**Our Commitment to Green Publishing**
Chelsea Green sees publishing as a tool for cultural change and ecological steward-ship. We strive to align our book manufacturing practices with our editorial mission and to reduce the impact of our business enterprise on the environment. We print our books and catalogs on chlorine-free recycled paper, using soy-based inks when-ever possible. This book may cost slightly more because we use recycled paper, and we hope you'll agree that it's worth it. Chelsea Green is a member of the Green Press Initiative (www.greenpressinitiative.org), a nonprofit coalition of publishers, manu-facturers, and authors working to protect the world's endangered forests and conserve natural resources.

*The Winter Harvest Handbook* was printed on Somerset Matte, a 10-percent post-consumer recycled paper supplied by RR Donnelley.

Library of Congress Cataloging-in-Publication Data
Coleman, Eliot, 1938-
  Winter harvest handbook : year-round organic vegetable production for
the twenty-first century / Eliot Coleman.
       p. cm.
  Includes bibliographical references and index.
  ISBN 978-1-60358-081-6
  1. Vegetable gardening. 2. Organic farming. 3. Greenhouse gardening.
4. Plants--Winter protection. I. Title.

  SB324.3.C664 2009
  635'.0484--dc22

2008053184

Chelsea Green Publishing Company
Post Office Box 428
White River Junction, VT 05001
(802) 295-6300
www.chelseagreen.com

To the children who love our vegetables.

"What business man, except a soil worker, will 'stop and talk' with a stranger? Who but a farmer or fruit grower or gardener will tell of his experience so fully and so freely, and so entirely without hope of gain? Who else will so frankly reveal his business secrets for the benefit of his fellows? Who else so clearly recognizes the fact that the world is large enough for all mankind?"

HENRY DREER
*Dreer's Vegetables Under Glass*


"One does not act rightly toward one's fellows if one does not know how to act rightly toward the earth."

LIBERTY HYDE BAILEY
*The Holy Earth*

# Contents

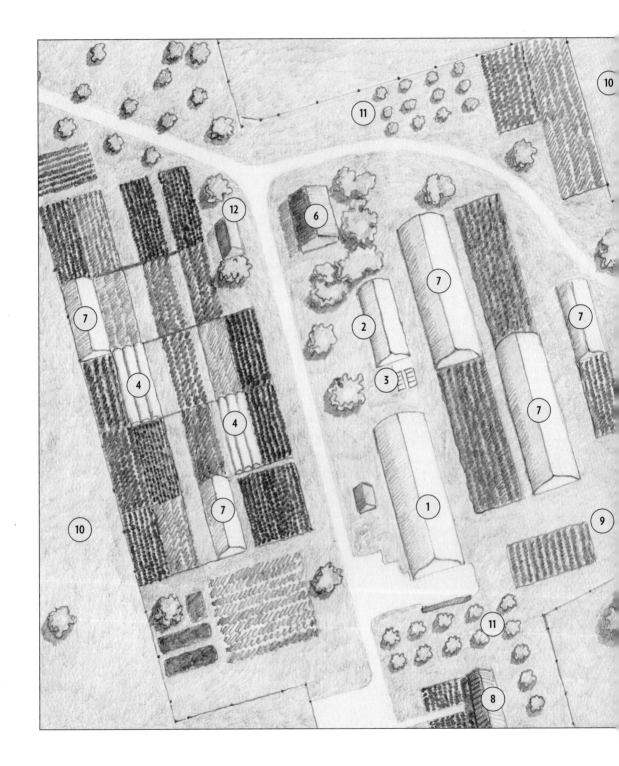

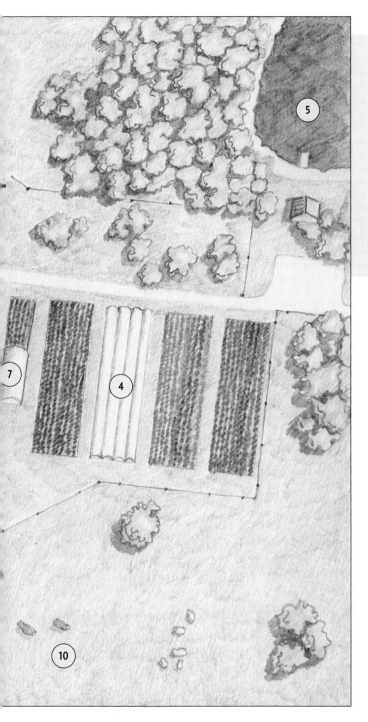

1. Cool greenhouse
2. Seed-starting greenhouse
3. Cold frames
4. Quick hoops
5. Irrigation pond
6. Work shop
7. Movable greenhouses
8. Farm stand
9. Herb garden
10. Pastures and hay fields
11. Orchard
12. Tool shed

# Introduction

Our farm in Maine is both traditional and nontraditional. We are traditional during the "growing season"—the summer months—when we produce fresh vegetables for sale. But we also produce fresh vegetables for sale during the winter months—the "back side of the calendar," so to speak. We achieve that winter harvest by growing cold-hardy salad and root crops in simple unheated greenhouses. Extending the season to the whole year (or at least most of it) means that we can hold our markets, keep our crew employed, and provide a more balanced year-round income. We believe our nontraditional winter vegetable production system has potential for growers in any part of the world where cold weather presently constrains production.

Our first serious investigation of the winter harvest began in the late 1970s. Simplicity, low external inputs, and high-quality outputs have always been the guiding criteria for any new project. Our goal was to find the lowest tech and most economical way to extend fresh-vegetable harvest through the winter months. Low-tech winter production began with old-time glass-covered cold frames and moved on to placing the frames inside simple greenhouses. That beginning evolved into larger, but almost as simple, 30-by-96-foot mobile greenhouses with an inner layer of lightweight row-cover material replacing the cold frames. The economics focused on seeing how much we could produce without incurring the cost of supplemental heat.

Since beginning commercial year-round production in 1995, we have recorded the evolution of our systems. This book describes the crops, the tools, the planting schedules, and the techniques we presently use to manage a four-season farming operation. It expands the instructions in our self-published pamphlet, *The Winter Harvest Manual*, and both supplements and updates the winter-harvest information in *The New Organic Grower* (revised edition, 1995). I have not repeated in this book material on important topics such as crop rotation, green manures, soil-block making, and so forth, that were extensively covered in *The New Organic Grower*.

These systems are not static. We are continually evolving them. We look forward to hearing from all those growers who will make great improvements in these systems and who will lead the way in the coming small-farm revival.

Eliot Coleman
Harborside, Maine
February 1, 2009

# chapter one

# The Winter Harvest

*. . . if we analyze their system, we see that its very essence is, first, to create for the plant a nutritive and porous soil, which contains both the necessary decaying organic matter and the inorganic compounds; and then to keep that soil and the surrounding atmosphere at a temperature and moisture superior to those of the open air. The whole system is summed up in these few words.*

—Prince Peter Kropotkin
*Fields, Factories and Workshops* (1898)

Our story begins with the winter season and the return of the sun. The crops we sell during the winter are not leftovers from traditional summer cultivation. They are, rather, part of a cycle of year-round production that emphasizes different crops in their respective seasons. Winter is the unique season of this uncommon small-farm model. In this book we lay out all the information gained from our experience that will launch prospective local growers into successful year-round production wherever they live.

Any claim about winter production of fresh vegetables in a cold climate with no heating or heat-storage systems seems highly improbable. One only has to glance outside in January to see how ragged or dead the plants in fields and gardens look. However, it's a misconception that all vegetable crops need summerlike temperatures for best growth. As inhospitable as cold temperatures may be for warm-season crops like tomatoes, that is not the case with those vegetables like spinach and lettuce or claytonia and mâche that prefer to grow in the cool seasons. Not only do many of them tolerate cold conditions and even temperatures well below freezing (as long as they are spared the desiccating effects of cold winter winds), they actually thrive and are sweeter, tenderer, and more flavorful.

In addition to the concern about cold temperatures, a second

To avoid confusion I should mention that British gardening books use the terms *cold* and *cool* greenhouses to refer to specific low temperatures. In the British nomenclature a cold greenhouse has a minimum temperature of 32°F and a cool greenhouse has a minimum temperature of 45°F. In this book I apply my own definitions to these terms: *cold greenhouse* describes a greenhouse that is unheated (although it can have a heater for times when you might wish to get an early start with a warm season crop like tomatoes), and *cool greenhouse* describes a greenhouse that is maintained at a minimum temperature of just above freezing.

I use the terms *greenhouse, high tunnel, tunnel greenhouse,* and *hoop house* interchangeably to refer to the pipe-frame, plastic-covered, translucent structures in which we grow plants.

misconception about winter growing is that day length is too short. Many people believe that supplementary lighting will be required. However, short winter-day length is not the barrier it appears to be. Crops do take longer from seed to harvest, but earlier succession planting across a wider range of dates can compensate for that reality. Most of the continental U.S. receives far more winter sunshine than parts of western Europe where, owing to milder temperatures, there is a long tradition of fresh winter vegetables. I'll discuss this in greater detail in chapter 5.

Planting crops in a heated greenhouse has always seemed the obvious solution for growing vegetables during the winter months. The old-time heated greenhouses for vegetable production were commonly called "hothouses." They were used for tomatoes at a minimum night temperature of 65°F (18°C) or lettuces at 55°F (13°C). An unheated greenhouse was considered unusable in cold winter climates, except as a storage area for hardy potted plants. Our successful experience with winter production proves that this is not so. We call our unheated greenhouses "cold houses" in contrast to "hothouses." In our cold houses there are many leaf and root crops that can be successfully grown and/or maintained all winter long.

Our economical cold houses are the end result of the quest we began in 1970 for simple, low-cost, user-friendly winter production. These unheated greenhouses are completely passive, much more so than the complicated and expensive "solar" greenhouse designs of the '70s. There is no heating system, nor any water or stone ballast with pumps or fans as a heat-storage medium, nor is there buried insulation around the perimeter. We followed our minimalist preferences and avoided any space-age materials, complicated technologies, or whizzing machinery with which we are not comfortable.

## Three Basic Components

The winter harvest, as we practice it at Four Season Farm, has three components: cold-hardy vegetables, succession planting, and protected cultivation.

**Cold-hardy vegetables** are those that tolerate cold temperatures. They are often cultivated out of doors year-round in areas with mild winter climates. The majority of them have far lower light requirements than the warm-season crops.

The list of cold-hardy vegetables includes the familiar—spinach, chard, carrots, scallions—and the novel—mâche, claytonia, minutina, and arugula. To date there are some thirty different vegetables—arugula, beet greens, broccoli raab, carrots, chard, chicory, claytonia, collards, dandelion, endive, escarole, garlic greens, kale, kohlrabi, leeks, lettuce, mâche, minutina, mizuna, mustard greens, pak choi, parsley, radicchio, radish, scallions, sorrel, spinach, tatsoi, turnips, watercress—which at one time or another we have grown in our winter-harvest greenhouses. (The most promising vegetables, those with which we have the most experience, are discussed individually in chapter 8.) The eating quality of these cold-hardy vegetables is unrivaled during the cooler temperatures of fall, winter, and spring. They reach a higher level of perfection without the heat stress of summer.

**Succession planting** means sowing vegetables more than once during a season in order to provide for a continual harvest. The choice of sowing dates, from late summer through late fall, and winter into spring, keeps the cornucopia flowing. In midwinter the vigorous regrowth on cut-and-come-again crops provides the harvest while late-fall-and-winter-sown crops slowly reach productive size.

We begin planting the winter-harvest crops on August 1, the start of what we call the "second spring." We continue planting through the fall. The reality of sowing for winter harvest is

Greenhouses and low tunnels protect fall crops as winter approaches.

that the seasons are reversed from the usual spring-planting experience. Day length is contracting rather than expanding; temperatures are becoming cooler rather than warmer. Success in maintaining a continuity of crops for harvest through the winter is a function of understanding the effect of shorter day length and cooler temperatures on increasing the time from sowing to harvest. Thus the choice of precise sowing dates for fall planting is much more crucial than for spring planting. The dates are also very crop specific, and I'll explain this in more detail in chapter 4.

We aim for a goal of never leaving a greenhouse bed unplanted, and we come pretty close. Within twenty-four hours after a crop is harvested, we remove the residues, re-prepare the soil, and replant. We keep careful records so as to follow as varied a crop rotation as possible.

**Protected cultivation** means vegetables under cover. The traditional winter vegetables will often survive outdoors under a blanket of snow. Since gardeners can't count on snow, the best substitute is shelter of an unheated greenhouse. Many delicious winter vegetables need only that minimal protection.

Our winter-harvest cold houses are standard, plastic-covered, gothic-style hoop houses. The largest of our houses are 30 feet wide and 96 feet long. They are aligned on an east-west axis. For the most part the cold houses need only a single-layer covering of UV-resistant plastic, whereas heated greenhouses benefit from two layers, which are air-inflated to minimize heat loss.

The success of our cold houses seems unlikely in our Zone 5 Maine winters where temperatures can drop to –20°F (–29°C). But our growing system works because we have learned to augment the climate-tempering effect of the cold house itself by adding a second layer of protection. We place floating row-cover material over the crops inside the greenhouse to create a twice-tempered climate. The soil itself thus becomes our heat-storage medium, as it is in the natural world.

Any type of lightweight floating row cover that allows light, air, and moisture to pass through is suitable for the inner layer material in the cold houses. The row cover is supported by flat-topped wire wickets at a height of about 12 inches (30 cm) above the soil. We space the wickets every 4 feet (120 cm) along the length of 30-inch-wide (75 cm) growing beds. The protected crops still experience temperatures below freezing, but nowhere near as low or as stressful as they would without the inner layer. For example, when the outdoor temperature drops to –15°F (–26°C), the temperature under the inner layer of the cold house drops only to 15°F to 18°F above zero (–10°C to –8°C) on average. The cold-hardy vegetables are far hardier than growers might imagine and, in our experience, many can easily survive temperatures down to 10°F (–12°C) or lower as long as they are not exposed to the additional stresses of outdoor conditions. The double coverage also increases the relative humidity in the protected area, which offers additional protection against freezing damage. The climate modification achieved by combining

inner and outer layers in the cold houses is the technical foundation of our low-input winter-harvest concept.

In a world of ever more complicated technologies, the winter harvest is refreshingly uncomplicated because all three of these components are well known to most vegetable growers. What is not well known is the synergy created when they are used in combination, and that is what we continue to explore on a daily basis on our farm.

## Mobile Greenhouses

We have added one new twist to a winter-harvest system by reviving an old European practice—the mobile greenhouse.

According to the best historical information I can find, the first mobile greenhouse was built in 1898 in England. Even though it was a large glasshouse, it could be moved safely because railroad wheels running on steel rails supported its iron framework. We have copied the mobile greenhouse concept, but on a far less expensive scale. I describe our mobile greenhouses in chapter 10.

Under the covers it looks like a perpetual spring.

The mobile greenhouse offers a number of advantages. First, it allows us to avoid the expense of having to cool the house when starting our winter crops in August. Instead, we sow winter crops out of doors in the field over which the greenhouse will move. Meanwhile the greenhouse continues to provide protection for heat-loving crops such as tomatoes, peppers, cucumbers, eggplants, melons, or sweet potatoes. We leave the greenhouse over the summer crops until the summer-crop season is finished, sometime in mid to late October here in coastal Maine. Then, we move the greenhouse to cover the winter crops. The following October, the same process takes place in the reverse direction.

This idea, protecting hardy winter crops with a second layer inside an unheated plastic greenhouse, was pioneered in the 1950s by E. M. Emmert, a professor of horticulture at the University of Kentucky. For some reason no one picked up on Emmert's innovation at the time: possibly because plastic greenhouses were so new; possibly because the concept seemed too good to be true. But it is more likely that growers were deterred by unfamiliarity with the day-length factor in winter gardening. Because of the slowdown in plant growth due to shorter days (coupled with cooler temperatures), winter crops have to be planted before winter. Timing the plantings is the key to success. The goal is to get plants almost to maturity before the day length becomes shorter than ten hours.

A second advantage of the mobile greenhouse is the avoidance of the buildup of pests, diseases, and excess soil nutrients, which can be problems in a permanent greenhouse. For one year out of every two, our growing beds are uncovered, exposing the soil to the cleansing powers of sun, rain, wind, and snow. As an additional advantage during the initial soil-building years, the uncovered year allows us to plant a long-term, deep-rooting, leguminous green-manure crop on that section. This green manure can occupy the soil of the uncovered site for as long as thirteen months (June through the following July), if you forgo a summer vegetable crop, or ten months (September through July) if you sow the green manure toward the end of the summer-crop season. The benefits of green manures for protecting, enriching, and aerating the soil were an important part of our soil-fertility-building program in the first few years. All green manures should be turned under three to four weeks before the planting date of the crops following them.

## Minimal Supplementary Heat

From the beginning of our commercial winter production we have had one large greenhouse equipped with supplementary heat. To distinguish this from our unheated cold houses, we call this a "cool house." We built the cool house because we knew a greenhouse would be the least expensive type of covered area for washing and packing our produce. One-quarter of the house has a concrete floor with space for our washing and packing facilities, our walk-in cooler, and for starting seedlings in the spring. Since we need to prevent our vegetable washing system from freezing in the winter, we installed a propane heater. The thermostat is set low, just above 32°F (0°C).

The remaining three-quarters of this house is used for growing winter crops. This was our laboratory for exploring the parameters of minimal heating. We learned that keeping this house just above freezing at night accelerates plant growth enough that we can harvest two more crops per winter than in the unheated houses (an average of five to six crops per year as opposed to three to four). When heating-fuel prices were low, one extra crop could pay for the cost of the propane to fuel the heater, so we came out ahead financially. We also discovered that with supplementary heat it is possible to keep highly popular crops like baby turnips and crisp radishes available all winter, whereas the freezing in the unheated houses limits their production. We could also bring our eagerly anticipated early spring carrots to harvest six weeks earlier (April 1) than in the unheated houses (May 15).

'Hakurei' turnips.

If a fuel source (such as wood) is cheap enough or local enough so that one additional crop can pay for the cost of minimal heat, simple economics suggests that we should add heat in all our houses. And indeed, the benefits we discovered, in addition to the possibility of getting an earlier start on warm-weather summer crops, convinced us to experiment with minimal heat for several

**Harvest Season of Cool-House Crops** From October to May in Zone 5

| Crop | Oct | Nov | Dec | Jan | Feb | Mar | Apr | May |
|---|---|---|---|---|---|---|---|---|
| Arugula | | | | | | | | |
| Beet, 'Bull's Blood' | | | | | | | | |
| Carrot | | | | | | | | |
| Celery | | | | | | | | |
| Chard | | | | | | | | |
| Claytonia | | | | | | | | |
| Endive, 'Bianca Riccia' | | | | | | | | |
| Lettuce | | | | | | | | |
| Mâche | | | | | | | | |
| Mizuna | | | | | | | | |
| Onion, green | | | | | | | | |
| Pak Choi | | | | | | | | |
| Parsley | | | | | | | | |
| Radish | | | | | | | | |
| Sorrel | | | | | | | | |
| Spinach | | | | | | | | |
| Tatsoi | | | | | | | | |
| Turnip | | | | | | | | |

**Harvest Season of Cold-House Crops** From October to May in Zone 5

| Crop | Oct | Nov | Dec | Jan | Feb | Mar | Apr | May |
|---|---|---|---|---|---|---|---|---|
| Arugula | | | | | | | | |
| Beet, 'Bull's Blood' | | | | | | | | |
| Carrot | | | | | | | | |
| Celery | | | | | | | | |
| Chard | | | | | | | | |
| Chicory, green | | | | | | | | |
| Claytonia | | | | | | | | |
| Endive, 'Bianca Riccia' | | | | | | | | |
| Leek | | | | | | | | |
| Lettuce | | | | | | | | |
| Mâche | | | | | | | | |
| Mizuna | | | | | | | | |
| Onion, green | | | | | | | | |
| Pak Choi | | | | | | | | |
| Parsley | | | | | | | | |
| Radicchio | | | | | | | | |
| Radish | | | | | | | | |
| Sorrel | | | | | | | | |
| Spinach | | | | | | | | |
| Tatsoi | | | | | | | | |

Early seedlings on the heated floor and late winter crops thrive in our cool greenhouse.

years. However, the original inspiration for the "winter harvest" was to see what we could achieve in winter *without* the complications and resource consumption of heating. Our success in the cold houses has been most gratifying, and they continue to be more than adequate for baby-leaf salads and braising mixes, spinach, leeks, Asian greens, winter carrots, and the spring crops that follow them. We continue to pursue the goal of doing as much as possible with unheated houses. Even though we have decided not to pursue the cool-house option further, I include in chapter 7 information from our experience for those growers who may find the idea appropriate to their operation. For growers in warmer climates than ours, the unheated houses will be all they need.

# chapter two

# Historical Inspiration

*In the vegetable department we have also several important things to learn from the French, and not the least among these is the winter and spring culture of salads.*

—WILLIAM ROBINSON,
*Parks and Gardens of Paris* (1869)

If year-round production of fresh local vegetables is your goal, and you like the idea of being small-scale and space efficient, then you will find no model more inspiring than that of the Parisian growers of 150 years ago. *La culture maraîchère* (market gardening) in Paris during the second half of the nineteenth century was the impressive result of years of improvement in both protected and outdoor vegetable production. The earliest developments in season extension (using primitive predecessors of the cold frame) had begun in the royal *potager* (vegetable garden) at Versailles under the celebrated head gardener La Quintinie in the 1670s and '80s. Those early beginnings reached their impressive climax in the hands of the Parisian *maraîchers* (market gardeners) between 1850 and 1900.

The "French garden system" (as it was called in English) was impressive for reasons that sound very up-to-date today.

- It was as local as you can get, taking place in and around an urban area. The cultivated land of the Parisian growers covered up to one-sixteenth (six percent) of all the land within the city limits of Paris. The Parisian street addresses given for some of these nineteenth-century "gardens" are the twenty-first-century addresses of office and apartment buildings. The city of Paris, once self-sufficient in fresh vegetables, must now import produce from far away.

- The selection of produce was excellent. This system fed Paris all year round with the widest variety of both in-season and out-of-season fruits and vegetables. Hotbeds heated with decomposing horse manure and covered with glass frames allowed the growers to defy the cold and produce fresh salads in January and early cucumbers and melons in May and June.

- The system was sustainable. Both the heat for winter production of vegetables in hotbeds and the amendments to maintain the fertility of the soil were by-products of composting another by-product—the horse manure mixed with straw that came from the city stables. This recycling of the "transportation wastes" of the day was so successful and so extensive that the soil increased in fertility from year to year despite the high level of production.

- A final impressive factor was the amazing productivity of the system as evidenced by the quantity of vegetables grown. In addition to feeding the inhabitants of Paris, the growers also exported vegetables to England. Growers averaged at least four and usually up to eight harvests per year from the same piece of ground. It was a successful system both practically and economically.

## Intensive Techniques

The average Parisian market garden at the time was between one and two acres in size. A leading grower gave the following as his first principle of success: "Always tend the smallest amount of land possible, but tend it exceptionally well." Another grower referred to the Parisian *maraîchers* as "goldsmiths of the soil" who knew the exacting techniques to create exquisite vegetables in any season. J. Curé in *Ma pratique de la culture maraîchère ordinaire et forcée* explained the situation thusly: "Intensive vegetable culture, that which one does in professional gardens with irrigation and compost easily at hand, differs from ordinary vegetable growing in the sense that it needs to be a successive process uninterrupted during the year, often with many different vegetables planted together on the same piece of ground" (author's translation).

The need to produce as much as possible from a small area resulted in intensive planting techniques that are hard for modern market gardeners to believe. For example, an early spring hotbed would be sown with radish and carrot seed broadcast and then transplanted with lettuces at the same time. The radishes would be harvested first, making more room for the carrots growing between the lettuces. The carrot tops would stick out from around the lettuces until the lettuces were harvested, which gave

**FRENCH SOURCES**

I derived the figure of 6 percent for the land area of Paris involved in vegetable production by dividing the approximately 10,000-hectare land area of Paris by the approximately 600 hectares that M. Courtois-Gérard states were in vegetable production in 1844.

The old French books that I consulted for this chapter are:

Courtois-Gérard. *Manuel pratique de culture maraîchère.* Paris: Librarie Scientifique, Industrielle et Agricole, 1844.

Curé, J. *Ma pratique de la culture maraîchère ordinaire et forcée.* Paris: Librairie Agricole de la Maison Rustique, 1904.

Gressent, Vincent Alfred. *Le potager moderne.* 12th edition. Paris: Librarie Agricole de la Maison Rustique, 1926.

Moreau, J. G., and J. J. Daverne. *Manuel pratique de la culture maraîchère de Paris.* Paris: Librarie de la Sociéte, 1845.

the carrots enough light and space to complete their growth. But as soon as the lettuces were harvested, young cauliflower transplants would be set out among the carrots. Once the carrots were pulled the cauliflowers had the frame to themselves until they were harvested and the ground was prepared for the next crops.

This level of intensive year-round production was powered by at least 100 and sometimes up to 400 tons of horse manure per acre, depending upon how many hotbeds were used. Decomposing manure was used for heat not only under the hotbed but was also filled into the walkways between the glass-covered frames covering the hotbeds to add extra heat. Once the hotbed manure had lost its heat and had broken down into crumbly compost it was shoveled out and used as a soil amendment. It has always been my experience that compost made from a mixture of horse manure and straw is the best of all for vegetable growing. The French *maraîchers* were strongly in agreement. Many growers at the time expressed the opinion that composted horse manure was the *only* suitable manure for vegetable growing.

These old *maraîchers* were also "organic" in the best modern sense, a conclusion they came to from practical experience. As long ago as 1870 Vincent Gressent wrote in *Le potager moderne*, an instruction book for Parisian growers: "For vegetable growing chemical fertilizers don't do all that one wants; they stimulate the plant and produce quantity, but to the detriment of quality. . . . In principle, insect pests only attack weak, sickly plant specimens lacking proper nutrition. . . . In proof of this I offer the market gardens of Paris where vegetable growing has reached perfection. . . . One does not see pest problems in Parisian market gardens wherever copious compost use and rational crop rotations are practiced by the growers" (author's translation).

In order to maximize production per square foot on these small production units, the access paths and walkways throughout the garden were only 10 inches wide, too narrow for wheelbarrow use. The manure (both fresh for generating heat and composted for fertility) was delivered to the beds in willow basket backpacks (*hottes*). These were woven with an extension of the basket that arched up and over the head of the worker

Classic old-time, glass-covered French hotbed heated by decomposing manure.

Woven willow basket backpacks (hottes) are used for delivering manure along the narrow paths of the French gardens to cold frames and hot beds.

so the load could be deposited where desired by bending far forward and letting the load of manure tumble out of the backpack over one's head. Horse manure from the city stables was brought to the gardens daily by the wagons returning from delivering crates of vegetables to the markets.

In addition to the heat generated by decomposing manure, additional climatic protection was provided by one-inch-thick mats made of rye straw, which could be rolled out over the glass covers for extra insulation on cold nights. According to a zone map published in the journal *Hardy Enough* (vol. 5, no. 4) the central part of France has a climate equivalent to that of USDA Zone 8. That would give Paris a winter minimum temperature range of 10°F to 20°F, but it was possibly a bit warmer owing to the heat island effect created by the city itself.

Crops not protected with cold frames were protected by 18-inch-diameter glass bell jars called *cloches* set close together in tidy rows. The *maraichers* used cloches for everything from starting transplant seedlings through protecting five mature

Workers unrolling straw mats for overnight insulation on a field of glass cloches.

heads of lettuce under each cloche up to harvest. Since each cloche had to be individually vented on sunny days (a small notched stick was used to prop up one edge) and since some growers had up to three thousand cloches, one can imagine the almost unbelievable amount of hand labor and attention to detail required. The cloches also could be covered with straw mats during colder periods.

## Transplanting the System to Britain

In 1869, British garden writer William Robinson was the first English-speaking outsider to enthuse in print about the quality of the produce and the skill of the Parisian growers in his book *Parks and Gardens of Paris*. He chided his countrymen for not adopting the superior French vegetable-growing techniques, but no one paid much attention at the time. When Prince Peter Kropotkin, the Russian anarchist revolutionary, praised the Parisian *maraîchers* enthusiastically in his book *Fields, Factories and Workshops* (1899), the gardening world began to take notice.

## WHICH CAME FIRST?

There is some fascinating background to the story of the British growers "discovering" French gardening techniques. I was encouraged to look further into the history of early intensive horticulture by a line in John Weathers' book *French Market-Gardening* (1909): "Some people are inclined to think that the present system of intensive cultivation as practiced in the market-gardens . . . in the neighborhood of Paris is an old English system that was dropped years ago and is now being revived." Joan Thirsk confirmed Weathers' comment in her *Alternative Agriculture: A History* (1997) in her discussion of the changes in vegetable production. "The greatest impact was made by the so-called 'French garden' which became the model for what was thought to be a wholly new style of market gardening on small acreages. . . . In fact, it was the seventeenth-century system revived and further modernized." Malcolm Thick describes that seventeenth-century system in *The Neat House Gardens: Early Market Gardening around London* (1998). It seems that out-of-season produce grown with cloches, frames, hotbeds, and extensive use of horse manure was common in London from 1620 to 1825. The area along the Thames known as the Neat House gardens was the most successful example of this thriving horticultural industry. Once the expansion of the city of London took over the land in 1825 (the gardens occupied what is now an inner suburb of London, a part of Westminster known as Pimlico) and the last gardeners moved out, it took only forty years for the knowledge of these intensive practices to fade from the general memory of British horticulture to the extent that someone as supposedly well informed as William Robinson considered French gardening a "new" system on his trip to Paris in 1865. I'm sure this is not the first time a change of land or circumstances has caused a once well-known gardening technique to be forgotten by subsequent generations until it becomes "new" when discovered again.

(Kropotkin referred to chemical fertilizers as "pompously labeled and unworthy drug[s].") And when a group of British market gardeners visited Paris in 1905, obviously wondering how French growers in basically the same climate were able to export salads to Britain all winter when the British weren't growing any, the interest surged.

The British growers were understandably impressed. Upon their return home they spoke in glowing terms about the great productivity of the French gardens. By chance there happened to be widespread interest at the time in helping unemployed factory workers return to being self-supporting on the land. Intensive vegetable production appeared to be the perfect way to do just that. A popular newspaper followed up its series of very upbeat articles by publishing an inexpensive how-to book, *The French Garden: A Diary and Manual of Intensive Cultivation*. A wealthy American businessman, Joseph Fels (of Fels-Naptha soap fame), who believed firmly in the benefits of small farming and of easier access for people to the land, bought six hundred acres at Mayland, Essex, England, to be turned into numerous mini-farms for intensive French-style production. His foreman, Joseph Smith, wrote one of the best instruction books, *French Gardening*, which contained an introduction by the aforementioned Prince Kropotkin. Other books followed rapidly, one with the title *Gold Producing Soil*, and most of them gave the impression that easy riches were to be gained through French gardening. As with other new horticultural "miracle" schemes, the hype was so extensive as to be detrimental to the outcome in the long run. Many French gardens in England failed through incompetence or did not live up to economic expectations. The high level of expertise needed for successful French gardening and the long hours of hard work involved were somehow lost in the glowing descriptions.

Although the system had a less than momentous influence on British market gardening (one commentator claimed it would never be successful because British growers would never work as hard as French peasants) it did eventually influence small-scale market-gardening techniques to some degree, if only rarely to the level of perfection that had existed in Paris. However, that was partially because the world was changing at the start of the twentieth century. The early days of tractors and chemical fertilizers were pushing agriculture into a preference for large-scale production. Automobiles were replacing the horse and buggy. By 1915 garden writers were noting the difficulties of finding sufficient horse manure and complaining about having to pay a much higher price when they could acquire it. Urban Paris was rapidly growing. Land became too expensive to keep in agriculture and was soon covered with buildings. The *maraîchers* moved to the outskirts of Paris but even there, as the twentieth century progressed, the growing suburbs soon priced them out. A great horticultural model eventually disappeared, but its techniques and inspiration were not totally lost. They remained alive in the old books and in the hands of a few growers who continued up to the end of the twentieth century.

## A Twentieth-Century *Maraîcher*

I was fortunate in the fall of 1974 to be able to visit a surviving example, or at least a close descendent, of this classic French system of intensive market gardening. Although nine miles south of Paris rather than within the city limits, the market garden of Louis Savier in Banvilliers showed clearly the influence of those earlier growers, both in the techniques used and the exquisite crops that resulted. Savier's two and a half acres was surrounded by a 6-foot-high wall, as had been true for each of the Parisian growers (south facing walls offer a warm microclimate). But in contrast to the nineteenth century, when other farms would have surrounded his small farm, suburban houses were Savier's neighbors.

That visit to Savier's garden was the most powerful influence on my development as a market grower. My handwritten notes begin with one word—"wow!" Quality was everywhere: the organized layout, the tidy closely spaced rows, the ranks of cold frames and hotbeds, the dark chocolate-colored soil and, most especially, the crops glowing with health. Even though I had begun my own market-garden career six years earlier and had read many books about intensive production, it wasn't until I stood in Savier's garden that I realized how well it could be done. I visited Louis Savier on three subsequent occasions prior to his retirement in 1996. Each visit was more impressive than the one before.

Savier had acquired the market garden in the early '60s from his father but had been displeased with the changeover to chemical inputs that had taken place during his father's lifetime. He

Louis Savier's farm.

returned to the age-old organic methods and then proceeded on to biodynamics and never looked back. He told me that pests and diseases had disappeared and crop quality had soared.

The crops that I listed in my notebook were lettuces (butter-head, crisp, and romaine), endive, escarole, mâche, radishes, leeks, carrots, celery, spinach, chard, turnips, onions, and parsley. Every bed was part of a planned crop rotation and included ingenious interplantings (leek/carrot, mâche/onion, radish/romaine) that took advantage of complementary maturity times and growth characteristics of the paired crops to produce impressive yields. The parsley was planted in out-of-the-way corners that might otherwise have gone uncropped and was harvested successively for three cuttings.

A unique feature of Savier's operation (one that had been

common in the Parisian gardens) was the space-efficient set of 30-inch-wide lightweight rail tracks (instead of roads) that gave access to all parts of the 2½ acres. Pushcarts ran along this rail track, one for delivering compost to the beds and one for moving crates of freshly harvested produce to the packing shed. A third rail cart carried the irrigation system. It had long arms sticking out to either side dispensing water through nozzles, and was self-propelled by water pressure as it towed the hose behind itself down the track.

Much of what was described in the old French books from the nineteenth century was still the same, but some had changed. Savier's garden included numerous glass-covered frames, but the labor-intensive glass cloches were no longer. Instead, glass and plastic greenhouses covered about one-quarter of the cropped area. Composted horse manure was still the fertilizer of choice, but the manure for heating hotbeds had been replaced by hot-water pipes. The average labor force of six workers per 1½ acres was still the same, but thanks to rototillers and faster transport to market, the 16-hour workdays of the Parisian growers had become more reasonable.

Savier figured he worked an average of 11 hours a day. When his suburban neighbors told him they worked only 8 hours a day, he would remind them of their average 3 hours per day commuting time (1½ hours each way). He told them he preferred to spend those 3 hours in his garden rather than in a car, bus, or train.

He was right, because this intensive market garden was a beautiful place to be. I remember one misty fall day in 1989 watching his daughter and one other employee on their knees harvesting and bunching 'French Breakfast' radishes, wearing waterproof pants with rubber bands close at hand on a belt dispenser, depositing the bunches in a line on the soil behind them ready to be crated and washed. The ease of organization of the work spoke of efficiency, but the colors and composition of the scene evoked a French impressionist painting.

The history of the old Parisian gardens is important because the factors that distinguished them and brought economic success to the nineteenth-century *maraîchers*—location, sustainability, quality, and productivity—are the factors that will bring economic success to the market gardeners of the twenty-first century. There is much to be learned from the techniques of the French *maraîchers* who worked with natural inputs to craft impressively productive systems. There is also much to be learned from the subsequent generations who have modified the old ideas with new technologies and labor-saving improvements without losing their commitment to flavor, nutritional quality, and the beauty of good work.

Harvesting 'French Breakfast' radishes at Savier's.

# chapter three

# Getting Started

*It is common sense to take a method and try it. If it fails, admit it frankly and try another. But above all, try something.*

—FRANKLIN DELANO ROOSEVELT

Like most fresh-vegetable enthusiasts, I have always wanted the production season to be never ending. That doesn't mean I long for an endless summer. I love the pleasures of fall, winter, and spring. I just want year-round freshly harvested food for my own and my customers' tables. I always knew that, somehow, there had to be a simple way to combine cold-hardy crops with a little protection during the cold seasons so I could produce food economically throughout the year even in the New England climate.

Cold frames have always been the simplest and least expensive climate moderator for the gardener of limited resources. I began using cold frames when I started as a grower in 1966, but I first started seriously developing these winter-harvest ideas from 1978 to 1981 when I ran an organic experimental farm just north of Boston, Massachusetts. I refined the system from 1982 through 1990 on a farm in a very cold area of Vermont. The fact that they worked just as well in those two different climates as well as subsequently here on the Maine coast convinced me of the wide applicability of winter production.

On trips to European farms during the 1970s, I had visited the few remaining practitioners of commercial cold-frame production of hardy winter vegetables in Holland as well as France. Their simple cold frames

## DUTCH LIGHTS

During the early years of my interest in the Dutch cold-frame design known as "Dutch lights," the following books were helpful:

Carter, A. R. *Dutch Lights for Growers and Gardeners*. London: Vinton & Co., 1956.

Quarrell, C. P. *Intensive Salad Production*. London: Crosby Lockwood, 1938.

Willmott, P. K. *Dutch Lights and Frames*. London: Ernest Benn Ltd, 1958.

Dutch light cold frames in Holland in 1978.

fascinated me because they did not employ highly technological solutions. To me, Styrofoam insulation, awkward reflective covers, and space-age materials seem inelegant. I am convinced that simpler is better, especially where simpler has been time-tested. Comparative investigations of different cold-frame designs show that the standard old-time model—a bottomless box made of 2-inch-thick planks, 8 to 12 inches high at the back and 6 to 8 inches high at the front, and covered with glass panels—is still the best. So I copied the Dutch design—approximately 30-by-60-inch glass panes in a wooden frame, (known as "Dutch lights")—because they were simpler to make than the French models I had seen at Savier's market garden.

## Adding the Second Layer

Those simple glass panes over bottomless boxes gave our plants a surprising amount of protection. Growing plants in a cold frame is the equivalent of moving them to a climate one and one-half USDA zones warmer, or about 500 miles to the south here on the East Coast. A cold frame will usually prevent the crops inside from freezing until the outdoor temperature goes below 25°F. But our winters get a lot colder than that, so in the winter of 1980, we used our imagination and took a chance. We had an unheated greenhouse constructed in a traditional Dutch style—a structural frame consisting of 2×4s and covered with the Dutch lights. We planted it with winter crops and erected cold frames inside over the crops. Voila! The great leap forward! Our plants moved an additional 500 miles to the south to a Zone 8 climate and, as icing on the cake, had a snow-shedding roof over them.

It is fascinating how one step forward will suddenly help focus your thinking about an overall concept. This was one of those moments. First, the simplicity of adding a second layer made me understand better what we were achieving. We were not actively battling against the cold of winter, as one is doing when trying to grow hot-weather crops in a heated greenhouse. Rather we were simply maintaining a *protected microclimate* sufficient for the needs of our hardy plants. It was like the difference between sitting inside by the fire on a cold day and being outside with enough layers of clothes on to keep you comfortable.

Second, we began to pay attention to how plant growth changed as the season progressed. Once past the middle of November, most of the crops no longer grew at summer speed. They were semi-hibernating, just idling their engines, so to speak, waiting for us to come and harvest them. In other words, we were not extending the *growing* season as one hopes to do in a heated greenhouse but, rather, we were extending the *harvest* season.

Those realizations really helped us turn the corner on developing this concept of winter vegetables in protected microclimates. Lacking a guide, at first we had to guess at when to plant. During our first few winters of experimentation, it was obvious that some of our crops were too small to be harvestable while others were too large to be as hardy as they ought to be to survive the winter days yet to come. (Younger plants are usually hardier than older ones.) We hadn't done too badly, but a lot more experimentation was necessary in future years in order to arrive at the ideal August, September, and October planting dates that would result in a productive winter harvest. Furthermore, we could tell that some of the crops would benefit from two, three, and even more successive planting dates so as to spread out the harvest better, and to take advantage of what slow growth did take place between mid-November and early February. Succession planting ensured that we would have more to harvest once the new year got well underway.

**Cold frames inside a hoop house.**
Photo by Karen Bussolini.

From that early beginning, the winter-harvest concept has blossomed. A few years experience gave us more precise knowledge about planting dates and determining when to add the inner layer. In addition, we experimented with making greenhouses movable. We devised basic systems for sliding hoop houses between two alternate sites. The first design relied on greased wooden skids sliding on wooden rails; another called for rails on the bottom of the structure, which rolled along on ball casters set in the top of support posts; a third had runners that slid directly along the ground like a sled; and a fourth had flanged wheels on the bottom of each hoop that rolled along pipes lying on the ground. (More on this in chapter 10.)

## Changing to Commercial Production

Up until the early 1990s, when we decided to pursue this idea on a serious commercial basis, our inner layer was the cold frames with which we had begun. However, we realized that in order to grow winter crops commercially, we had to find an inner layer that was less expensive and more time-efficient. (Cold frames are costly to build and need to be manually vented so they won't overheat on sunny days.) After a winter of trials, we could easily see that the obvious choice to replace the glass was floating row cover held a foot above the soil on flat-topped wire wickets. Although row covers did not provide quite as much climatic protection as the cold frames had provided, row covers were self-venting, lighter in weight, easier to place over or take off the crops, and much less expensive.

Similarly, we knew we should shift production to larger greenhouses than our early prototypes, and we decided upon 30-foot-wide-by-96-foot-long houses as the most efficient choice. We had never moved greenhouses that large before, but by using our metal sled-runner design, and pulling them with a tractor just as one would pull a large sled, we had greenhouses that moved reasonably easily and could be bolted securely to ground anchors once they were in place.

At the start of our foray into winter production we joked about how it might be possible to run a "backwards farm," producing salads and main-course vegetables from October 1 to May 31, and then taking a long summer vacation. So, for a number of years, we tried winter-only growing. We were curious to learn what was possible if we concentrated all our energies on the unexplored potential of winter. The reality was not quite as good as the dream. There was indeed a whole new eight-month harvest season, but vacation time was limited to the second half of June (after cleaning out the greenhouses) and the first half of July (after which the work of preparing everything for the season to come actually begins).

We grew green manures during the summer season to boost the soil up to high production standards. We also worked on refining many of the unique greenhouse design and cropping programs that I present in this book. Our present year-round schedule is the result of combining all we have learned from summer-only and winter-only growing into a system that supplies the best of both. In chapter 4, I'll explain all the details about how our schedule ebbs and flows throughout the year.

'Space' spinach.

## Customer Response

Another dimension of the winter harvest is the quality that it offers to our customers. Their appreciation is the most gratifying we have known in many years as professional growers. People love having access to food harvested fresh either that day or the day before on a local farm—in the middle of winter! Over the past few years a flurry of articles have appeared in newspapers and scientific journals confirming what everyone's mom always knew: "Vegetables are good for you!" Government nutritional recommendations exhort us to eat five servings of fruits and vegetables daily. Customers tell us that our winter-harvest products make it easy for them to eat vegetables.

- First, the taste, the sweetness, and the just-harvested freshness are exceptional. Their children *ask* them for our raw carrots. One woman told us that she used to suffer all through the winter looking forward to fresh summer vegetables. Now, she said, she tolerates summer looking forward to eight months of intensely flavorful winter production.
- Second is convenience. Our salad mix has been referred to as a healthy fast food, "because it looks so inviting you want to eat it, and is so easy to put a handful into a bowl and add dressing that you do just that."
- And third is the fact that it is grown locally during the winter months. Customers say winter doesn't seem so long or bleak when they can always look forward to our next locally grown delight.

For our part, we can now participate in all the seasons of Nature's cycle, and we enjoy farming as an ongoing process, not just the start-and-stop operation it was when we were only summer growers. And remember, this is happening in Maine. Over 85 percent of the U.S. is further south than where we are and has more sun and warmer winter weather. There's nothing standing in the way of winter production of high-quality fresh produce in any part of the country, except perhaps lack of knowledge about how to employ the simple technology of cold houses and row covers and lack of experience in planning planting schedules for continuous production.

# chapter four

# The Yearly Schedule

*O Winter, ruler of the inverted year.*

—WILLIAM COWPER

For the first six years of our commercial winter-harvest production we sold vegetables only from October 1 through May 31 ("the other eight months" as we referred to them). In addition to a baby-leaf salad mix our cold-house crops included carrots, spinach, mâche, leeks, and scallions, plus tatsoi, pak choi, and other Asian greens. From the cool houses we had radishes, turnips, turnip greens, Swiss chard, watercress, parsley, and arugula. From storage there were onions, garlic, shallots, winter squash, celery root, parsley root, scorzonera, and storage beets. In spring both the cold and cool houses provided early crops of arugula, carrots, baby beets, baby new potatoes, broccoli, fennel, kale, lettuce, turnips, and overwintered onions.

Those six years helped us focus on developing the new concepts of the winter harvest, and it was time well spent. We worked on refining many of the unique greenhouse-design and cropping programs that this book discusses. We were aware, however, that to achieve the economic potential of the small farm we would need to reincorporate summer production in the future. And so we did by adding tomatoes, peppers, eggplants, and cucumbers in the greenhouses, and artichokes, beans, cabbage, cauliflower, celery, melons, peas, radicchio, summer squash (in addition to many of the crops listed above) in our outdoor fields.

The next few years, during which we ran full production both summer and winter, were truly exhausting. It is difficult to work at the flat-out speed that small farming demands for twelve months a year with no break. Although the economic returns were in favor of summer crops (our gross for the four summer months was slightly above that for the eight winter months) we were very aware that the winter months contributed importantly to the summer by getting our crops ready earlier in spring thus allowing us to establish ourselves in new markets in addition to keeping hold of our regular markets after the summer season ended. At present we reconcile all of these factors by scheduling a four- to five-week vacation for our crew and ourselves at the time when plant growth, customer interest, weekly income, and our energy levels are at their lowest ebb—late December to late January.

## Fall and Winter

We achieve this by timing our end-of-summer/early-fall sowing dates to maximize fall greenhouse production from November 1 right up through December 21. (We can successfully harvest many crops from outdoor fields until the end of October.) That allows us to sell everything we can possibly grow in the high-demand pre-Christmas market. In addition we have simplified our production during the winter months. At present, spinach, sown in mid-September, is the only multiple-harvest overwintered green crop we grow. We harvest the spinach so heavily to meet the December demand that it needs a month to recover before the first new-year harvest in late January. In order to save labor we don't do mesclun in fall but grow head lettuce instead. As we harvest the once-and-done greenhouse crops in November and December (lettuce, radish, turnip, baby pak choi, celery, fennel, scallions), spaces open up and we re-prepare and resow them to crops that will start maturing from mid-February on. Thus by the end of December we have picked all the crops that were sown for fall harvest and have replanted the greenhouses to crops that will be ready for the late-winter/early-spring harvests to come. Our four- to five-week vacation commences at the winter solstice.

During the years when we experimented with adding minimal heat to our largest greenhouses (see chapter 7) we were able to keep producing a far wider variety of crops than just those avail-

Spinach in a cold house before being covered for winter.

able from cold houses during the first two months of the new solar year that begins after winter solstice (the most difficult period for a cold-house grower). We were proud of the variety and quality we could offer and pleased to be able to consistently supply our customers every month of the year. However, our records show that expenses were at their highest (due to fuel costs) and yields were at their lowest (due to slow growth) during those weeks.

There was also another disadvantage. In order to be able to harvest during those weeks we needed a good bit of greenhouse space dedicated to crops sown for January/February harvest, which meant that we had less to sell in November/December. By aiming greenhouse production as we do now to maximize the November/December sales and running all our greenhouses as cold houses, we sell just as much but cut way back on expenses and hassles. During the five weeks after winter solstice there are just our "candy carrots" and overwintered leeks to harvest and sell fresh (until we run out of them in mid-February) but we are able to hire someone to do that for us during our vacation.

## The Dependable Spinach Crop

Overwintered spinach has become our major winter green crop for three reasons. First, it is the perfect winter green for the cold houses. Spinach continues producing new leaves all winter unlike, say, kale, another cold-hardy crop, which stops new growth during the cold months. Second, it is an enormously popular winter crop and the demand is always more than we can supply. And third, the timing is perfect for the crop rotation we use in that mobile greenhouse. Mid-September-sown outdoor spinach is hardy enough not to need protection until the season is over for the summer crops in the greenhouse. We then move the house over the spinach during the second half of October. We start harvesting around Thanksgiving (our spinach harvest comes from the field through the end of October and from another greenhouse during November), and each bed will provide four harvests at about monthly intervals before the spinach starts thinking about going to seed in late March. After the final harvest, we clean up and prepare the beds for an early-April transplanting of our earliest tomato crop. At that point what was a cold house all winter becomes a warm greenhouse because we turn on a propane heater that has sat dormant all winter so as to maintain a 60°F night temperature for the tomatoes.

## Crop Rotation

We aim to harvest at least three crops per year from every square foot of the cold houses—two in winter and one (or more) in summer. A typical rotation in one of the 48-foot cold houses might include a winter-harvested carrot crop followed

Succession plantings for mid-winter harvest in our cool house.

on March 15 by planting the first of the baby new potatoes. After harvesting the potatoes, we would transplant a summer crop of Charantais melons in late May. After we cleared the melons the house would be planted to a fall-harvested spinach crop. Then in late November we would move the house to cover a later-planted spinach crop for spring harvest.

In another 48-foot cold house we might have grown a rotation of fall stir-fry crops and early spring lettuce. Following those we would set out six-week-old tomato plants on May 10 and protect them with an inner layer. Once it was safe to remove the inner covers, the tomatoes would be trellised to the overhead supports to keep them productive as long into the fall as possible. A green manure of red clover might be undersown in the standing tomatoes on September 1 and the tomato vines would be unclipped

from the overhead supports the day before the house was due to be moved to cover a winter crop of carrots in late October. This rotation would repeat a second year on the uncovered site before being exchanged with a different rotation in another house for the subsequent two years.

With the supplementary heat in a cool house we can plant and harvest four crops and sometimes even five during the winter months alone, and we always grow heat-loving crops in there over the summer. Since the cool-house crops are almost evenly divided between the lettuce family (Compositae) and the cabbage family (Brassicae) we make sure that they are alternated with each other in addition to alternating with the warm-weather crops (cucumbers, peppers, eggplants) in order to have as complex a rotation as possible.

**Spring in the cool house.**

Our original cool house is nonmobile. Therefore we are very particular about soil preparation, quality of compost, crop rotation, and irrigation in order not to create pest problems or accumulate excess salts. We have succeeded in keeping that house highly productive for fourteen years thus far. Growers need to be aware that soil problems in greenhouses years ago were what spurred interest in the first movable greenhouses. It was traditional to dig the soil out down to 16 inches deep and replace it with new field soil when problems arose. The pioneers of movable greenhouses realized that it would be far less work to move the greenhouse, and I will talk more about that in chapter 10.

There is no single perfect crop rotation or yearly schedule in this business. The differences in markets, climates, and growers' preferences assure endless variations. And that is what makes exploring the winter harvest so stimulating to the agricultural imagination. I know many growers who have started with a greenhouse just to get a jump on spring, then used it

Tomatoes continue growing in the mobile green-house while winter crops have just been planted outside.

to extend production into the fall. Next they explored planting even earlier spring crops, and eventually became four-season growers. They all talk about how involved they have become with the thinking and planning required for pursuing new crops and new cropping sequences. Farming in the summer months is fascinating, but farming for twelve months is even more so.

# chapter five

# Sunlight

*Thus, though we cannot make our sun stand still, yet we will make him run.*

— Andrew Marvell

After a few years enough people had heard about our "new" idea to bring out the naysayers. "But you can't do that," they said. "You may be able to give protection from cold but there isn't enough winter light for plants in New England. You need to be somewhere like the south of France if you plan to garden all winter." They were astonished when we informed them that the city of Portland, Maine, on the "sun-baked Atlantic coast of Maine," as we now jokingly call it, lies on the same parallel of latitude as the warm sandy Mediterranean beaches of St. Tropez, France; that New York City shares the 41st parallel with Naples, Italy; that Washington, D.C., on the 39th parallel, lines up with the Mediterranean island paradises of Majorca and Corfu; and that all parts of the U.S. below the 37th parallel (the northern borders of North Carolina, Tennessee, Arkansas, Oklahoma, New Mexico, and Arizona) experience the same day length as northern Africa.

In an article I once read in a British gardening magazine, the author emphasized the key role of the sun for winter gardening. Britain, he said, had a maritime climate that makes it in most respects a gardener's dream. But, the author stated with a sense of resignation, despite the moist, temperate British winter weather, the short winter-day length was an enormous obstacle to vegetable growing. Britain, he noted, is located "up there with the polar bears."

Despite the low sun angle and long shadows, there is adequate midwinter sunshine in the U.S.

## Latitude and Day Length

Polar bears? What does Great Britain have in common with polar bears? A lot, it turns out. A quick consultation of a world atlas proves the statement is more than justified. The southern tip of Great Britain sits just above the 50th parallel of latitude. If you follow that parallel across Europe to Asia and then to North America, you'll see that it runs through cities we would consider "the far north"—Kiev, Ukraine; Ulaan Goom, Mongolia; Moose Jaw, Saskatchewan; and Seal Cove, Newfoundland. All of those places are some seventy miles further north than the U.S./Canadian border, which follows the 49th parallel of latitude. Travel a few hundred miles even further north into the heartland of Britain, and you will be on the 54th parallel, the same latitude as Great Whale River, Quebec, on the shores of icy Hudson Bay. Thus an English vegetable gardener who tills a plot near Leeds or Manchester would experience the same winter-day length as would polar bears on the hunt for dinner in Hudson Bay.

But our farm in Maine is nowhere near polar-bear latitude. It is on the 44th parallel, the same as Avignon, France, and Genoa, Italy. On this side of the Atlantic, the 44th parallel passes through Eugene, Oregon, and Oshkosh, Wisconsin. Because we're on the same parallel of latitude as these cities, the same *sun line*, so to speak, we all have the same day length and the same potential amount of winter sun. And because the French and Italians appreciate the value of fresh local food so highly, winter production of hardy crops is a common affair even in regions at far higher latitudes than we are. For example, the renowned winter cold-frame vegetable production around Paris that I described in chapter 2 took place along the 49th parallel.

Of course, the climate in France and Italy is milder than ours, thanks to the Gulf Stream. Our colder temperatures probably explain why U.S. gardeners have failed to take advantage of our more-than-adequate winter sunlight.

In our experience, the period during which plant growth slows down significantly begins when day length drops below ten hours (in early November at our latitude). This is the point at which the overall light energy available diminishes to the extent that it significantly affects the rate of plant growth. Growth remains slow until early February, when the plants resume growing vigorously in response to the day length becoming longer than ten hours and overall light energy becoming adequate again. In order to be able to continue succession harvesting throughout the coldest months, plants must reach a certain minimum size before day length drops below the ten-hour mark. In other words, to be dependably productive for winter harvesting, crops need to make sufficient growth in the fall. Even the true winter annuals (such as mâche, claytonia, spinach, etc.) are slow to get started if sown during the short days of late fall and early winter. This is the biological imperative that drives us to figure out precise timing of planting dates for our fall and winter crops.

At our Maine farm (44.33° north latitude, 68.58° west longitude), the winter days are shorter than ten hours from November 5 to February 5. For those on the 39th parallel, like Washington, D.C., the dates are November 17 to January 24. For Charlotte, North Carolina, on the 35th parallel, the period of day lengths under ten hours extends from December 1 to January 10. Atlanta, Georgia, just above the 33rd parallel, experiences a short-day period from Dec. 7 through January 5. Once one gets to the 32nd parallel, which runs from Savannah, Georgia, to El Paso, Texas, and then south of San Diego, California, the shortest winter-day length never drops below ten hours. Comments by the eminent British greenhouse researcher W. J. C. Lawrence confirm our experience that the ten-hour day provides a reasonable yardstick for measuring the slowdown in winter plant growth. From his greenhouses at Merton near London on the 51st parallel, Lawrence reported in *Science and the Glasshouse* (1948) that plant growth slowed during the period from October 27 to February 16 when days are shorter than ten hours. We think the winter harvest could be successful as north as Anchorage, Alaska on the 61st parallel even though at that latitude they experience a day length less than ten hours from October 16 to February 24.

## Mythology and Day Length

Asian greens, like this mizuna, are excellent winter crops.

Humans have long had their own way of understanding the changes in day length and its affect on agriculture. Early Greek farmers, whose practical experience added mythical stories to astronomical fact, knew intimately that the power of the sun and the length of the day are the principal influences on agriculture. They created the myth of Persephone to explain the effect of winter conditions. As the story goes, the earth goddess Demeter had a daughter, Persephone, who was abducted by Hades to live with him as his wife in the netherworld. Demeter would have nothing to do with this and threatened to shut down all plant growth. Zeus intervened and brokered a deal whereby Persephone would spend only the winter months with her husband, Hades. Demeter, saddened by her daughter's absence, made the earth barren during that time. On our farm we refer to the period when the days are less than ten hours long as the Persephone months.

The pagan agricultural calendar in the British Isles brings this ancient awareness closer to our hemisphere. It is often called the Wheel of Life. We are all familiar with four points on that wheel—spring equinox (March 20/21); midsummer, or summer solstice (June 21/22): autumn equinox (September 20/21); and midwinter, or winter solstice (December 20/21). Most people, however, are less aware of the agricultural significance of four other dates on the wheel. These are the cross-quarter days, which are evenly spaced between each of the four dates above. Each date marks a festival.

'Rouge d'hiver' lettuce.

The first of these festivals is called Imbolc. It takes place on or about February 2. It celebrates the growing of the light, the onset of lactation in ewes about to give birth, and Brigid, the goddess of fire and fertility. Traditionally, fires were lit to represent the increasing power of the returning sun. Next in order, on May 1, is the festival of Beltane. It marks the beginning of the summer pastoral season when grasses for livestock begin to grow again, and the lushness of summer is off and running. The third festival of the year, celebrated on August 1, is called Lughnasadh, the first day of fall in the pagan calendar. Lughnasadh marks the beginning of the harvest season and the ripening of the first fruits. Around November 1 comes the last of these four festivals, Samhain. This celebrates the start of winter and the last of the harvest.

When one farms with nature as we do, it is easy to notice how closely the dates and meanings of these early Celtic celebrations fit in with our practical experience and day-to-day work. For example, February 1, the date of the festival of Imbolc, is the time of year when more rapid spring growth begins in our greenhouses as the Persephone period draws to a close. We have noticed that outdoor transplanted vegetables begin their season of rapid growth right about May 1. And August 1 is truly our bounteous harvest time. Almost every crop we grow is in full production on that date. It is also the start of our fall planting season for winter crops. And November 1 is the end of our outdoor-harvest season and the beginning of the next Persephone period when growth slows down for winter.

## Charting Growth Patterns

In order to develop a calendar of accurate planting dates for weekly winter harvests, we have compiled tables of time-from-seeding-to-harvest for many crops based on our notes over the years. They all show a reasonably similar pattern: the time from planting to maturity *doubles* for an early February (Imbolc) harvest in a cool house (minimally heated greenhouse) and *triples* in a cold house. What does this pattern tell us? It indicates that limited sunlight, while important, is only one of the factors that cause plant growth to slow down during the winter. The effect of below-freezing temperatures is also significant.

This graph is a reasonably accurate depiction of the effects of lower light levels and lower temperatures on a crop that would normally take 40 days from seed to harvest. The curves show the increasing and then decreasing number of days to harvest from fall through winter to spring in a cool house and a cold house. Compiled from data collected for 12 years (1996–2008) at Four Season Farm, Harborside, Maine.

The graph on page 49 shows an example of a crop that takes 40 days to mature for either a September 1st or June 1st harvest. That same crop requires 80 days from sowing to maturity for a midwinter harvest in a cool house and 120 days in a cold house. The pattern described is similar for most all the winter crops we have tried. You can use a graph like this one to calculate the number of days in advance to plant in order to harvest at any particular date on the horizontal axis. For example, to plan this crop for a March 15 harvest in a cold greenhouse, you would find the point where March 15 lies on the cold-house curve. From there, you would trace down to a number on the horizontal axis.

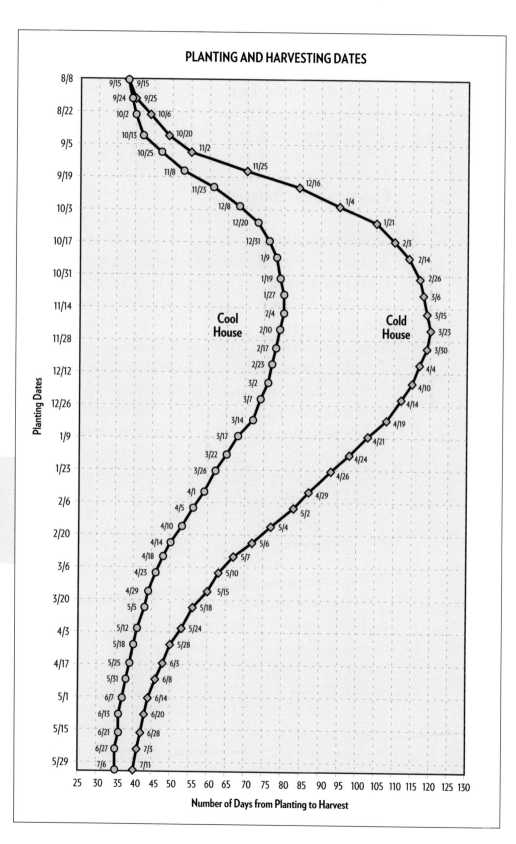

PLANTING AND HARVESTING DATES

That number (118) means that you would want to plant 118 days before March 15 (i.e., November 17) for a March 15 harvest. Gardeners at a higher or lower latitude than ours (approximately the 45th parallel) should increase or decrease their expected days to harvest based on the ratio between the day length at their latitude and ours. Days to harvest will be longer at higher latitudes and shorter at lower latitudes. The National Weather Service Web site offers instant day-length calculations for any location—www.srrb.noaa.gov/highlights/sunrise/sunrise.html.

This scheme is the most accurate way we've devised to translate our personal experience with days-to-harvest into data that others can use. Someone competent with a computer should eventually be able to turn information like this into a program that would allow growers to type in the desired date of harvest, the normal days to maturity of the crop, their latitude, and possibly their greenhouse night temperature, and the computer would compute the planting date. We encourage all growers to collect data on their farms and compare theirs with others' experiences to see if such a program would be reasonably accurate.

Cut-and-come-again winter crops like spinach, chard, claytonia, and tatsoi continue productive regrowth after harvest throughout the Persephone months, as long as they have well-established root systems. The cutoff point for new sowings is the end of October. After that time, seeds of these crops will germinate, but will grow very slowly. The seedlings just sit there waiting expectantly. Once the ten-hour day returns in February, their growth speeds up. Those sown first will mature first as the season progresses.

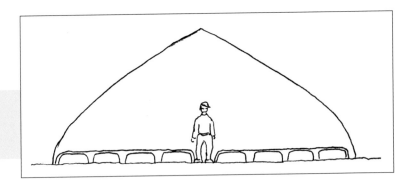

Double coverage moves the covered area about three USDA zones to the "south."

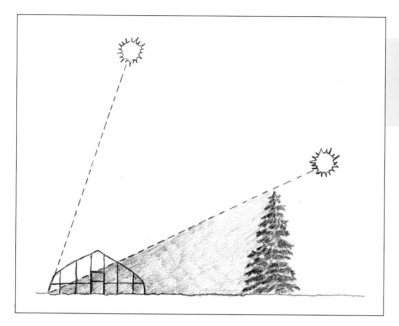

Make sure your greenhouse location won't be shaded when the sun is lower in the sky in winter.

## Layers, Light, and Temperature

Replanting right through the winter, as spaces open up follow-ing harvest, is an important part of our system. This would be impossible outdoors during a Maine winter, of course, but we do it consistently in our cold houses. The soil under the inner layer of our cold greenhouses experiences no more than light surface freezing even on the coldest nights. That might seem surprising, but it's not when you recall that our method of twice-tempering the microclimates of the beds gives them the equivalent of a Zone 8 climate. (See the frost-depth map in appendix A.) With the possible exception of one or two days each winter, when an extremely cold night is followed by a heavily clouded day, the soil in the beds is always unfrozen by 10 AM and ready to rake into a fine new seedbed for replanting. This diurnal (happen-ing in the daytime) influx of the sun's heat, which warms the covered beds above the freezing point during the day, is the key to successful winter production in our cold houses.

During a January 1996 research trip along the 44th parallel in France and Italy, we saw tunnel greenhouses everywhere, many with smaller tunnels inside them. The growers were adding that second layer to get a slightly earlier start with tomato and pepper

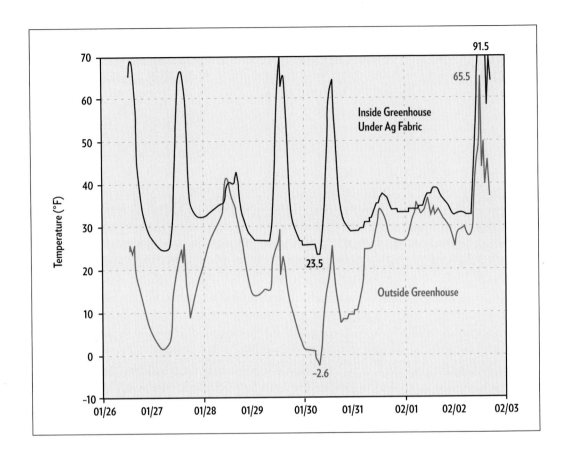

crops. They told us it was well worth the trouble because an unheated greenhouse with inner tunnels gave 6° to 7°F (3.5°C) of freeze protection. The temperature records we keep at our farm are in line with their experience. But our records also show an additional benefit that would not be apparent to those who are only concerned with maintaining above-freezing temperatures for an early start with tender crops. The effectiveness of the inner layer increases progressively as the ambient temperature drops. That 6° to 7°F (3.5°C) of protection inside the double-protected tunnel when the outside temperature is 25°F (–4°C) increases to 30° to 35°F (16° to 19°C) when the outside temperature drops to –15°F (–26°C). The above graph comparing inside and outside temperatures shows that the protective

'Bull's Blood' beet leaves.

blanket of the two layers becomes dramatically more effective just below the point at which tender crops freeze.

Out of curiosity we asked all the European growers we visited if they ever worried about whether there was sufficient sunlight to produce salad crops in winter. They were surprised by the question, as might be expected, because their salad crops were healthy and beautiful. They told us the difficulty was not day length but cold weather. We had to chuckle at that statement because compared to their 40°F to 45°F (4° to 7°C) average January temperature, we are growing in a climate with a 21°F (−7°C) average January temperature. They were astonished by what we had to contend with. It has been interesting to note, when we have visited parts of the U.S. (see map 1 in appendix A) with the same or warmer January average temperature as Provençal and Tuscan growers enjoyed, that there has been almost no winter vegetable production in high tunnels in those areas. We have wondered if it is fear of cold, the lack of a winter vegetable-growing tradition anywhere but Florida and California, or the fear of competition from those traditional winter vegetable areas. It may also be the knee-jerk association in North America between the word *greenhouse* and the word *tomato* to the almost total exclusion of cool-weather crops.

# chapter six

# The "Cold" Greenhouse

*Don't fight forces; use them.*

—BUCKMINSTER FULLER
*Shelter* (1932)

Making two visits to one of our cold houses—one at dawn after a below-zero night, and the other a few hours later—provides a striking introduction to the winter harvest. During the dawn visit all the crops are frozen solid. Raising the inner covers, which is difficult because they too are frozen, reveals a spectacle of stiff, frost-coated leaves bleak enough to convince anyone that this idea is foolhardy. Yet a few hours later, after the sun (even the wan sunlight of a cloudy day) has warmed the greenhouses above freezing, the second visit presents a miraculous contrast. Under the inner covers are closely spaced rows of vigorous, healthy leaves that stretch the length of the greenhouse. The leaf colors in different shades of greens, reds, maroons, and yellows stand bright against the dark soil. It looks like a perpetual spring.

Over the course of devising, developing, and improving our winter-harvest practices, we have amassed a collection of technical studies on hardy crops and the effect of freezing temperatures. Copies of research papers on all aspects of greenhouse growing fill our file cabinets. Yet none of them offer as much information (or inspiration) as those two visits to the cold house.

## Hardy Crops

In the natural world, hardy crops like spinach and chard inhabit niches where resistance to cold is a requirement for survival. Winter-annual crops, like mâche and claytonia, have found their space to grow by germinating in fall, growing over winter, and going to seed in spring. Whereas the outdoor winter climate

## ACTA HORTICULTURAE

The Dutch journal *Acta Horticulturae* was very valuable when we were first researching the subject of greenhouses for unheated out-of-season production. *Acta Horticulturae* publishes papers on horticultural subjects delivered at research symposia throughout the world. Go to the Web site www.actahort. org and then to the list of volumes under the section "Commission Protected Cultivation." You can read the abstracts online and then either join the International Society for Horticultural Science to read the full articles online or find the books themselves. They are most likely to be available in the library of your local land-grant university.

here in Zone 5 Maine is too harsh for even the hardiest of these crops, the twice-tempered climate under the inner layer of our cold houses offers them conditions within the range to which they are adapted. See appendix B.

Even after working with this unheated system for many years, I continue to be amazed by the daily miracle. The same three words keep coming to my mind every winter day—*unheated, uninsulated, unbelievable!* When you enter the protection of one of our cold greenhouses, you can take off your parka because the microclimate you encounter is that of a location approximately one and one-half USDA zones to the south. When you reach your hand under the row covers you have moved another one and one-half zones south where the Maine winter definitely does not prevail. Outdoors the climate is Zone 5; under the inner layer, the climate is Zone 8.

We started using the phrase *cold house* to describe these structures because the word *unheated* made it sound as if we are not doing something—heating—that we should be doing. Furthermore, it may be clearer to use the descriptive phrase *high tunnel* or *cold tunnel* and avoid the word *greenhouse* altogether since many people assume that greenhouses, if unheated, are expensive superinsulated technological marvels or complicated heat-storage devices. Ours are neither. The best short statement to describe our approach is the epigraph to this chapter by Buckminster Fuller from his book *Shelter* (1932)—"Don't fight forces; use them." Instead of bemoaning the forces of winter and trying to fight them head on, we have limited our intervention to the climatic protection provided by two translucent layers. Instead of the usual thinking, which only sees greenhouses as a way to grow heat-loving crops during cold weather, we have said, "So it's cold. Great! What vegetables thrive in the cold?" The answer is some thirty or so hardy vegetables.

Fighting force requires energy, and energy costs money. Our cold-house approach takes advantage of everything our two translucent protective layers can get for free from the sun as well as the residual heat of the soil mass and then works within those limits. The same applies in reverse during the summer. When the protected microclimate inside the houses turns warm, we don't fight that warmth with motorized greenhouse cooling systems. We use it to grow heat-loving crops.

## The Outer Covering

When we first started growing crops in cold houses, we covered all of the houses with just a single layer of plastic. We made that choice to maximize light input. Using two layers of plastic and blowing air into the space between them to inflate the plastic provides more protection from cold, but it also cuts out an additional 10 percent of available light. Also we prefer to work with systems that are inexpensive and simple. Thus, we decided to forgo the expense of the second layer and the electric blower required to inflate the layers.

We are interested in comparing greenhouse plastic from different manufacturers to find the type of cover that lets in the most light and keeps in the most heat. In our cold climate we want to increase daytime heat gain and light levels, so we favor covers that maximize those inputs. Plastic covers are available with an anti-drip coating that causes condensed moisture to form a thin film instead of droplets. Covers with this type of coating not only let in more light but the thin film of moisture also acts to reflect back the heat waves radiating from the soil at night thus helping to keep the air inside the house warmer. Growers in the southern states where cold is not as intense may want to use plastics designed to block infrared input and thus help to keep the greenhouse from overheating.

## Using Double Covers

For experimental purposes, we trialed one small air-inflated house (17 feet by 36 feet) without heat. The temperature records we kept show that nighttime low temperatures averaged 4°F (2.2°C) warmer in the air-inflated house than in a cold house with a single-layer outer covering. For example, on a cold night, when the low temperature was −8°F (−22°C) outside, the temperature dropped to 2°F (−17°C) inside a single-layer house and 20°F (−7°C) under the inner layer of row cover. By comparison, in the air-inflated house, the low temperature was 7°F (−14°C) and 24°F (−4°C) under the inner layer of row cover.

Our observations of crops during this trial showed some interesting comparisons between the two houses. Although we could detect no apparent difference in the quality of the crops of harvestable size, we did notice faster growth of new seedlings in the air-inflated house in winter. That house also warmed more quickly on cold mornings because the layer of sunlight-blocking frost that forms on the inside of the plastic melted off more slowly in the single-layer house. Based on this trial, we began double-covering the cold houses where we would be sowing new crops from December 15 to February 15. With the rest of the cold houses, such as one that protects leeks for midwinter harvest, we continue with our inclination in favor of simplicity and better light input and use only a single sheet of plastic to cover the house.

## The Inner Layer

The success of our work with cold frames and then row covers convinced us of the benefits of the inner- and outer-layer concept. We wondered if we could do even more. We thought about placing smaller tunnel greenhouses inside the larger ones as some Japanese farmers were doing, but, on further consideration, we decided that the management and ventilation seemed complicated and the use of space seemed inefficient. We considered motorized night-curtain systems of reflective material, which are sometimes used in heated greenhouses, but they were very expensive. After exploring all of the above, we reverted, as we usually do, to the simplest, least expensive option—a floating row cover as the inner layer. If we had started our winter operation with more elaborate systems, we never would have known if they were really necessary.

Although we worried that floating row covers might be considerably less protective against cold than glass cold frames, the self-ventilating nature of the row covers and their availability in large sizes were overwhelming advantages. And, further, we did not know if we had yet pushed our crops to the lowest temperatures they would tolerate in a protected microclimate. Our opinion, after many years of practical experience with winter-harvest systems, is that the protected microclimate we have created is successful principally because it protects against wind (think of wind-chill readings and the desiccating effect of cold dry winds on winter vegetation) and, secondarily, because it protects against the fluctuating wet-dry, snow-ice conditions of the outside winter. In this microclimate, a few degrees of temperature one way or the other does not appear to be the crucial determinant of survival for most of our crops.

## MORE ON EMMERT

One day, shortly after we began investigating these winter-harvest ideas, we stumbled across a journal article in the library referencing the early work with plastics in horticulture by a University of Kentucky professor, Emery Emmert. It was a fascinating find and reinforced my belief that every supposedly new idea in agriculture has been explored before by someone else. Dr. Emery Myers Emmert (1900–62) is acknowledged as the father of plastic greenhouses in this country, but his accomplishments went far beyond that. During the 1950s he pioneered row covers, plastic mulch, and inner layers in unheated winter houses as well. His field greenhouses and row covers were the models for today's high tunnels and low tunnels. As you can tell from the following list of publications he was a tireless experimenter.

Emmert, E. M. *Low-cost Plastic Greenhouses.* Lexington, KY: Kentucky Agricultural Experiment Station Progress Report 28, 1955.

———. "Plastic Row Covering." *Market Growers Journal* 85, no. 4 (1956): 40.

———. "Plastic Mulch for Vegetables." *Kentucky Farm and Home Science* 2, no. 1 (Winter 1956): 8, 9, 11.

———. "Black Polyethylene for Mulching Vegetables." *Proceedings of the American Society for Horticultural Science* 69 (1957): 464–69.

———. "Earth Helps Heat Greenhouse: Lettuce Grows Unharmed in Below-Freezing Weather." *Kentucky Farm and Home Science* 7, no. 2 (Spring 1961): 4–5.

### Easy Handling

We plan to put the row covers over the crops just before the weather gets cold enough to freeze inside the greenhouse. One of the delights of using row covers inside a greenhouse is the ease of management. Since there is no wind, there is no need to bury or weigh down the edges. Even large pieces can be removed and replaced easily for harvest and other access needs without worrying about them being caught by a gust of wind.

For the large houses our interior covers are 20 feet wide by 50 feet long, large enough to cover one quadrant of a 30-by-96-foot greenhouse. The 48-foot houses are covered by two pieces each 15 feet wide. The covers are supported, 12 inches above the soil, by flat-topped wire wickets. We make the wickets from 76-inch-long straight lengths of number 9 wire. The flat top is 30 inches wide, the same width as the beds, and each leg is 23 inches long. Thus, when the wickets are in place, they do not block the access path between the beds.

We space the wickets every 4 feet along the length of a bed, which provides sufficient framework to support the row-cover fabric. When the fabric is in place, we pull it taut and clip it to the end wickets of the quadrant with clothespins. That prevents the fabric from sagging under the weight of condensed moisture, which can be quite substantial. We have noticed occasional frost damage at points where the fabric has drooped down and frozen to the leaves below, as opposed to no damage when the fabric does not touch the plants. The edges of the fabric drape down over the edge of the wickets and rest along the side of the greenhouse or in the pathway.

### Some Revealing Comparisons

In order to learn how much protection we would sacrifice by shifting to fabric covers from our original cold frames, we conducted trials using two types of spun-bonded row-cover fabrics, one lightweight and one heavyweight. We compared them to one another, and we also compared the results of using them alone against using them in combination with an aluminized cloth cover, which is totally opaque to sunlight. This cloth

Clothespins hold fabric to wickets.

is used as night-curtain material in heated green-houses because it reflects back 100 percent of the long-wave radiation emitted by the soil at night, thus trapping the heat. Plastic-based materials such as the row-cover fabrics are transparent to long-wave radiation.

The results of the trial made it easy to decide against using the aluminized cloth. During the trial, we laid the aluminized cloth over the row-cover fabric every evening and removed it every morning. We expected the aluminized cloth to increase the temperature under the covers, and it did, averaging 3°F warmer nighttime minimums than the row cover alone. However, we detected no differences in crop quality as a result of the warmer minimums. Since the cost of the aluminized material is very high and the twice daily spreading and removing were a great deal of extra work (especially on mornings when it was frozen to the row cover material beneath it), all for no increase in crop quality, it clearly was not worth adding to our system.

The difference with and without the aluminized cloth would

be greater without some help from the natural world. A film of moisture condenses on the floating row covers at night, and this film is nearly opaque to long-wave radiation and provides a reasonably reflective surface. Thus, it acts to prevent heat being radiated through the row covers as it would when the row covers are dry. There is usually plenty of humidity under the covers when they are covering crops of harvestable size. It is only when we have cleared a crop, worked in more compost, and reseeded that the soil surface can dry out and the air can be less moist. We find we can get around this to raise the night temperature a few degrees and benefit the young seedlings by moistening the surface soil if it looks dry. A buried water line with frost-proof hydrants makes water available inside our large houses and within 100 feet of all the others.

The comparison between a lightweight and a heavyweight spun-bonded fabric provided us with some intriguing insights. The heavyweight fabric we trialed is three times heavier than our standard lightweight fabric. It seemed logical that a heavier fabric would have more insulating value and keep the covered area warmer at night. At the start of the trial, the minimum nighttime temperatures under the heavy fabric were a degree or two warmer than under the lightweight. However, the heavy fabric only allows 50 percent of sunlight to pass through as opposed to 85 percent for the lightweight fabric. That meant the heavyweight fabric inhibited the crucial daily rewarming of the protected area under the fabric. The results, after a couple of days, were colder minimum temperatures and more soil freezing under the heavier fabric. This trial made clear that this is a sun-run system. The most important factor is the daily influx of sunlight. Not only does the light fuel plant growth, it also adds heat to the soil—heat that we can capture with the inner covering and thus raise nighttime temperatures. In this case less is more, and we now use only the lightweight fabric.

We have also compared the standard spun-bonded fabric with a Japanese row cover made of polyvinyl alcohol (PVA), which we were able to get from a California importer. This material had many pluses and some minuses. It is extremely durable and should last up to eight years under our protected conditions compared with only a year or two for the spun-bonded fabrics. PVA allows 90 to 92 percent light transmission. It has also averaged nighttime temperatures one degree warmer than the spun-bonded fabrics. Unfortunately the PVA cover cost about five times more per square foot than the spun-bonded fabric. Also, it was available only in a 78-inch width. We solved that problem by taking the fabric to a local sail maker who, for a reasonable price, sewed it into coverings wide enough to span our cold-house quadrants. In the end though, the fact that the PVA fabric was not locally available and required sewing made it seem more trouble than it was worth, and we decided to just use the spun-bonded fabrics.

Throughout our experimental investigations of greenhouse plastics and materials for the inner layer, our goal was to push the limits of the unheated system. We have opted for less expense, better light transmission, and simplicity over better temperature protection even though we farm in Maine. Those decisions may seem backwards for a winter-harvest system in our climate, but the crops have been surprisingly resilient. Nevertheless, we don't think we have found the ultimate answer yet. We continue to search for ways to provide more adequate protection for crops while trying to determine the best balance between extra effort expended in management and labor and improved results in growth and quality.

## The Role of Daytime Highs

We expect there may also be a cumulative effect from more substantial night protection. Warmer soil temperature resulting from more effective nighttime cover during the cold months should maintain both higher nighttime air temperature and a faster rate of plant regrowth. However, it may be possible to achieve a similar effect by allowing higher maximum daytime temperatures to occur. Normally we begin to vent our houses when the daytime temperature under the inner layer reaches

70°F. We have thought about venting at a lower temperature so the plants would experience a narrower range of temperatures, which intuitively seems as if it would make sense in the winter. But we have one small house with inadequate ventilation that gets much warmer (85° to 95°F) during sunny winter days. This house also experiences higher nighttime temperatures, which may be attributable to increased soil heat storage during the day. Thus far we have not detected any difference in crop quality (better or worse) as a result of the higher daytime temperatures.

Some studies of plant physiology suggest that rate of plant growth is not affected by the daily highs and lows but rather by the average temperature over twenty-four hours. If that is so, then, following a 20°F night, a 90°F daytime temperature might be better than a 70°F daytime temperature—a 55°F average over twenty-four hours rather than a 45°F average. We have a lot of hunches but no hard opinions yet on any of these variables. We plan to investigate these ideas further in future years.

Another significant biological reality of growing cool-weather crops in winter greenhouses is that *too warm* is

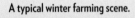
A typical winter farming scene.

more damaging to these winter-harvest crops than *too cold*. On our farm the transition period to begin thinking more about too warm rather than too cold is late February. At this point, even though the row cover fabric that we use for the inner layer is self-venting, it may not vent the heat quickly enough. We heed the soothsayer's caution to Caesar and "beware the ides of March" because by March 15, at the latest, we need to begin folding back the inner covers in the cold houses on sunny days to prevent overheating of the crops beneath. Growers in warmer climates will need to figure out their own critical date: one guideline is to begin monitoring overheating shortly after the end of the Persephone period in your region.

March is also the month when we plan to start irrigating again, whereas, because of low evaporation and high water tables, we have had to provide little supplemental moisture during the winter months.

## Summing Up

Obviously, growers in climates with less severe winter weather can grow a wider range of crops in cold houses than we can because the duration, depth, and frequency of temperature drops will be less. They can similarly create protected microclimates for the same winter crops we grow with fewer resources than we require. Growers in the warmer sections of Zone 8 and in Zone 9 (see map 2 in appendix A) could get by with row covers alone in areas with little snow. Based on our experience and the temperature records we have kept over the years, we think that growers in Zone 7 would find they could succeed perfectly well solely with unheated houses. Growers in the milder parts of Zone 7 might even find a double-covered, air-inflated high tunnel sufficient protection without the row-cover inner layer. However, they might want to have a small heater in reserve for spot protection on exceptionally cold nights (which is a reasonable option for any grower and achieves protection with minimal resource use).

For growers in Zones 3 through 6 we recommend trying everything from additional inner covers to specializing in spinach, mâche, leeks, claytonia, and Asian greens (the hardiest crops) in the coldest months of winter. The crops and the systems that work best will not be the same in all situations. The climate maps in appendix A provide a number of yardsticks by which to compare winter climates in other parts of the country. For comparison, we are located about two-thirds of the way up the Maine coast.

The eventual solution for an ideal winter-production system may come either through finding better inner- and outer-layer materials or through managing some greenhouses with minimal heat (see the next chapter) and some as cold houses. We still think increasing light transmission by a few percentage points is more important than raising nighttime low temperatures by a few degrees but, to be honest, we do not really know whether light level makes as much difference when temperatures are low in midwinter and the crops are basically hibernating. As other growers begin exploring these ideas it is our hope that there will be unrestrained exchange of ideas, techniques, and new information. The cold houses are the challenge that led us into this work in the first place, and we expect that they are where the most exciting new innovations will be developed.

# chapter seven

# The "Cool" Greenhouse

*When it's cold outside, I got the month of May.*

— S. Robinson and R. White, "My Girl"

Our minimally heated greenhouses are our "cool houses." Cool houses offer options for midwinter growing and marketing beyond those of the cold houses. However, once you begin adding heat to a greenhouse and get "the month of May," you're on a slippery slope. With incrementally more heat you can have the months of June or July or August and make the move into the "hothouse" realm. Many greenhouse growers have followed that path and grow only tomatoes or cucumbers. That was never our intent. We have always been interested in growing a wide range of hardy winter crops that could fully supply our local markets and using the minimal amount of energy to do so.

We began researching the potential of a just-above-freezing cool greenhouse in order to increase the variety of our winter production. As I described in chapter 1, we were using one end of a greenhouse for washing and packing produce, and we set the thermostat at 35°F (1.5°C) so as to protect our water supply from freezing in winter. The results we saw with the vegetables growing in the rest of that house—twice as many *harvests* per winter compared to the unheated houses and a wider selection of crops—caught our attention.

We have continued to set our cool-house thermostat at a just-above-freezing temperature because that has proven adequate for the cropping options we wish to explore. Yes, by adding heat we are going against Buckminster Fuller's advice not to "fight forces," but we have tried to determine the least costly way to do it.

We think of the minimal heat in the cool house as a different kind of protective layer. From another perspective, we

Beds are continually replanted in a winter greenhouse.

can compare our minimal-heat system to the developments in energy-saving design for automobiles—the hybrid versus the pure electric model. Some auto researchers have determined that for the best overall efficiency, the combination of an electric motor with a small gasoline motor is a better choice than the electric-only model. We have been interested in determining whether, for the economic success of a four-season farm in our climate, the combination of unheated greenhouses *and* minimally heated greenhouses would provide a better income and a more competitive position versus the shipped-in imports.

We have taken the logical steps to make the cool houses efficient. They are double-covered (two layers of plastic with an air-inflation fan). According to greenhouse research, that 4-inch dead-air space between the layers of plastic can lower our fuel consumption by up to 40 percent. Also, we make sure the houses are tight and the doors and vents fit well to prevent cold air infiltration.

Is the just-above-freezing temperature at which we set the thermostat the lowest nighttime greenhouse temperature that will assure success with the midwinter crops we wish to grow? Could they tolerate an even lower temperature without losing ground? We continue to investigate this question. Our sense based on some informal trials conducted in the early '90s is that there may be no damage to most of these hardy crops as long as the minimum temperature doesn't drop below 26°F (−3°C). (We ran these trials in an experimental greenhouse using a radiant heater and a wide-range thermostat.) This has also been our experience with outdoor crops. The occasional spring frost below 26°F is when we have noticed cosmetic damage on hardened-off early lettuce or broccoli transplants, whereas they seem unaffected by temperatures above that level. However, on a few occasions when heaters have malfunctioned, we have also noticed that temperatures just below freezing, although resulting in no cosmetic damage, do slow down growth for up to a week after the freeze. Thus, from the point of view of increasing winter production, a dependable nighttime minimum above 32°F (0°C) makes sense.

## Adding More Heat

Once we began to explore minimum heat we put heaters in 60 percent of our greenhouse space because the demand for our produce constantly exceeded the supply. We realized that we could achieve the equivalent growing area of a whole new greenhouse simply by adding heat to one of the cold houses, because the added heat would allow us to double the number of winter harvests in that house. The cost of a heater is much less than the cost of a new greenhouse. Furthermore, we didn't have to worry about covering and maintaining an additional greenhouse, and we could make better use of the fertile soil we had already worked so hard to create. In addition, as tough as we may think we are, we also appreciated

A beautiful pack of bunched 'Tinto' radishes in one of our homemade boxes.

the better working conditions in midwinter in a house where we could raise the temperature if we wanted to.

In addition to increasing the level of production in winter, the above-freezing nighttime temperature in the cool houses also increased the variety of crops we could grow during the colder months. For example, popular crops such as turnips, radishes, 'Bianca Riccia' endive, and arugula are not available for quality harvest during December, January, and February in the cold houses. However, these crops are successful in the cool houses and, being cool-weather crops, their quality is outstanding. In the future, we may find cultivars and/or passive protection techniques that will be successful for these crops in the cold houses throughout winter, but we have not found them yet.

Lettuces for the Christmas market in a cool greenhouse.

## Heating Options

During the early trials, standard propane-fueled greenhouse heaters warmed our cool greenhouses. These heaters are smaller than would be required if we needed to maintain a 65°F (19°C) night temperature in midwinter for a crop like tomatoes. But are there other options that make practical and economic sense at the moment? We have recently installed a large wood furnace in our washing and packing greenhouse to replace the propane heater (except during exceptionally cold weather), and it is a reasonable improvement. We have priced a wood-fired hot-water boiler system that could warm all the cool houses, but the initial cost would be ten times as much as we have spent on propane heaters. In addition, unless it was a self-feeding wood-chip system, we would have to spend a lot of time loading the furnace at night. We continue to look for renewable solutions. There are exciting recent developments in using very hot-burning wood furnaces to heat hot water during the day. The water is stored in large insulated tanks and drawn on to heat the greenhouse at night. These systems avoid the air pollution and creosote buildup of damped-down wood fires and the need for keeping the furnace fueled for twenty-four hours a day.

We have friends who have built an ingenious system that burns used cooking oil directly for greenhouse heating. (Information on the design and their experience with the system is available at www.laughingstockfarm.com). We envy growers in more temperate parts of the country where these heating concerns are not an issue.

Our experience thus far is based on the very simple unheated systems we started with and the minimally heated systems we have been trialing. Two other options for winter production are adding artificial lighting to create longer days and installing warm-water pipes in the soil to raise soil temperature. We have not experimented with artificial lighting because it would add another major use of energy and because no light bulb can truly duplicate sunlight. It seems to us that if we use incomplete, artificial light, there would be something missing in the quality of the resulting produce.

We have been slow to investigate soil heat for the same reason. We try to keep our production systems as natural as possible, and we can think of no situation in the natural world where agricultural soils are warmer than the air above them in midwinter. However, from the point of view of improving crop growth and complementing an air-heating system, soil heat has much to recommend it. The soil temperature, even in our minimally heated houses, drops to 42°F (6°C) at the 4-inch depth by midwinter. Some evidence suggests that lettuce growth does not slow down in winter because of shorter days—lettuce can only use eight hours of light—but because of the cooler soil temperatures. Thus, warming the soil seems a logical step for winter production. In addition, greenhouse studies have shown that soil heating can supply about 20 percent of the total heat needed by a winter greenhouse depending on the desired greenhouse temperature and the crops to be grown. We wonder whether a soil-heated greenhouse with wickets and an inner layer would keep the area under the row covers above 32°F (0°C) at night without having to heat the air above. If so, or if almost so, that could save a lot of money on the fuel bill for minimal heating.

All of our trials in the cool houses and all of our speculations about how to do it better are fascinating, but we remain content with our decision, as mentioned earlier, not to continue in that direction. We now add minimal heat to only one small growing area where we still do a few trials, but we may end even that. The challenge of the simple, minimalist, unheated production is where our hearts lie and where we will concentrate our efforts.

One minimal heating option we did seriously consider but haven't tried is the "earth tube" concept. A smooth-walled, rigid plastic pipe with a 12-inch diameter is buried about 6 feet deep for 100 feet across a field and then into to the greenhouse. A fan would draw outside air through the pipe. At that depth, the air would be warmed to the temperature of the earth—45°F (7°C). The air would then be blown under the inner layer down the length of the greenhouse through perforated plastic tubes. According to research, the energy use by the fans would be about 15% of that required to create the heat artificially.

# chapter eight

# Winter Crops

*My vegetable love should grow,*
*Vaster than empires, and more slow.*

—ANDREW MARVELL

## Salid Mix

Baby-leaf (mesclun) salads are an ideal crop for the winter harvest since immature leaves of the salad crops are far more cold tolerant than mature ones. Our mix has included red lettuces, green lettuces, broadleaf arugula, sylvetta arugula, endive, narrow-stem chard, claytonia, minutina, spinach, mâche, watercress, and beet leaves. All are carefully chosen, naturally hardy, winter-salad varieties. As we state in our advertising, based on nutritional data from the U.S. Department of Agriculture, this salad blend contains at least 5 times more calcium, 4 times more iron, 12 times more vitamin A, and 6 times more vitamin C than a salad of head lettuce.

Quality should be the primary concern of any baby-leaf salad grower. We work hard to *set* rather than just follow the quality standards. We don't sell salad mix ingredients that are too large, or bitter, or tough, or stringy, or frost damaged. If we are not completely satisfied, we leave that ingredient out of the mix until conditions improve. These evaluations have led us to move some crops for midwinter harvest in the cold houses, such as claytonia, from the colder edge beds to warmer inner beds; to do more succession plantings of some crops like minutina and narrow-stem chard so as to have more new young leaves coming along rather than relying on regrowth; to cut back some other crops earlier—red-oak lettuce, for example—because the regrowth is hardier than the initial leaves; and to continually do trial plantings of both standard and potential crops so we

Our colorful baby-leaf salad mix.

can identify cultivars better suited to our conditions, in addition to finding new flavors, shapes, and textures for the mix.

Our mix is composed only of whole baby leaves that are washed, mixed, and packed directly after harvesting (as described in chapter 15). Ideally, leaves are no more than three inches in length. We believe a quality mesclun must have leaves that easily fit onto a fork and into the mouth. We have seen salads sold locally containing mizuna leaves with seven- to eight-inch-long stems. In our opinion, overgrown leaves are better consigned to a braising mix or sold bunched as cooking greens.

Maintaining our quality and size standards is not easy, because we also do not chop mature plants into small pieces like the cut-up endive and radicchio seen in supermarket mixes. Instead, we grow an Italian endive cultivar, 'Indivia Bianca Riccia da Taglio' (white curly endive for cutting), sold by Johnny's Seeds as 'Bianca Riccia', which has nice light-colored frilly leaves at the baby-leaf stage.

We haven't yet found a radicchio that we like for baby leaves, but we actually prefer 'Bull's Blood' beet leaves for red color, and so that's what we grow. The cool conditions of our winter greenhouses intensify the beautiful deep maroon, and the flavor does not have radicchio's bitter edge (which under poor growing conditions can become so bitter as to ruin the whole salad). Cool winter temperatures keep arugula and water-cress from becoming too strong and biting. In fact, we purposely do not add the usual hardy oriental greens to our salad mix because our customers prefer a salad without the mustard tang. Many parents have told us this is the only mixed salad their children will eat because they prefer the milder, cool-weather flavors of our ingredients. We sell the hardy oriental greens along with spinach and 'Bull's Blood' as a separate braising mix (see page 78).

There are three components of our winter mix—lettuce, endive, and arugula—that do not consistently meet our quality standards once temperatures get too cold for too long. We have traditionally given them a little protection in our cool house during January and February. Although we have found some lettuce varieties, principally the oak-leaf types, that are very cold hardy at the baby-leaf stage, their quality during parts of January and February is better from the cool house than from under the inner covers of the cold houses. The same is true for 'Bianca Riccia' endive and standard arugula. The wild arugula sold as 'Sylvetta' is perfectly hardy, but we need to learn more about its soil-fertility needs and timing of planting to make it as successful as we know it can be. At times, we have sold salad mixes without these three ingredients, and our markets have accepted them. However, we prefer to sell a consistent product. So we have continued to grow these three in a cool house while pursuing our search for hardier cultivars and for the best warmth-conserving inner- and outer-cover combination.

Despite our preference for producing a consistent salad mix with the same percentage of each leaf type every time, reality occasionally intrudes in winter. Extreme weather, poor germination, or poor quality of certain crops can cause us to modify the quantities of the different ingredients. The farthest overboard we have gone was one mix that was 50 percent claytonia, and another that was 50 percent baby spinach. A nearby upscale restaurant with its own winter greenhouses found itself with only claytonia available for a two-week period one January and used it with great imagination. It would appear that both our and their customers are adventurous enough to be forgiving of occasional slips. The key is to maintain a high quality standard even when your consistency slips off the rails for a brief period. See appendix E for a chart of sowing dates for a succession of fall and winter salad harvests.

## Braising Mix

Our braising mix is made up of a preponderance of hardy Asian greens. We cut the leaves slightly larger than our baby-leaf salad but never more than 4 inches long unless we are desperate. Our choice of varieties for the braising mix excludes any leaves that are not normally cooked. That rules out mâche, lettuce, claytonia, and endive by our standards. The mix includes spinach and chard in addition to all the Asian greens (mizuna, mibuna, tatsoi, pak choi, tokyo bekana, etc.). We tried the red-leaved mustards but none of them have sufficient color in winter, so we use the 'Bull's Blood' beet leaves instead. Spinach is not necessary if the tatsoi supply is good, but we do like the chard leaves for their tenderness. Many customers have told us they like this mix for a raw salad as a change of pace, so we sell it as an Asian salad/braising mix.

The possibilities for experimenting with winter mixes are nearly endless. One thing to figure out is how much of each ingredient you need to plant to meet demand and how often to plant to get the harvest timing right. Another is gauging how the plants will react to cold conditions—whether their quality will remain high, and how soon they will bolt to seed.

## Experimental Mixes

We did a trial one year to see what crops could be planted later in the fall to supply a baby-leaf Asian salad or stir-fry mix in mid-February, the coldest time of our winter. We planted a broad selection of oriental greens on October 25 in one of our

### STIR-FRY PAK

One winter we took advantage of the hardiness of Asian greens and their culinary possibilities by putting together a main-course item we called the "Stir-Fry Pak." This was a 10-by-15-inch cellophane bag containing the following whole ingredients: a head of 'Mei Qing Choi' pak choi, a head of young tatsoi, one 'Shunkyo' semi-long pink radish, one 'Hakurei' turnip with greens, one 'Tadorna' extra-hardy leek, and a large carrot. The beauty of the contrasting colors and shapes of root, stem, and leaf plus the customers' pleasure at finding all the ingredients in one bag made our "Stir-Fry Pak" a market success, so successful in fact that the trial plantings sold out by mid-December before the mature leafy greens got a true cold-weather testing. However, we know the tatsoi, leek, and carrot can withstand our coldest conditions and we continue to experiment and learn more about the others.

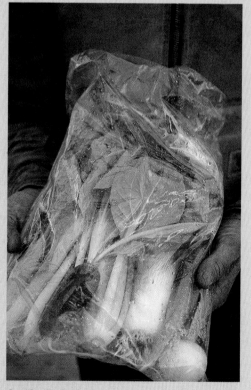

Our "Stir-Fry Pak"—all the ingredients sold together in one easy-to-purchase bag.

unheated houses. On the 15th of February we harvested a salad mix consisting of 4-inch-tall plants of the most successful cultivars. They included 'Joi Choi', 'Yu Choi' (edible rape), 'Mei Qing Choi' (baby pak choi), tatsoi, and mizuna. They all need to be harvested promptly at that stage because within a week afterwards all but the 'Joi Choi' started to go to seed. The 'Joi Choi' continued to grow, and we sold them bunched as "baby pak choi" until the end of March.

The February 15 salad mix also included some very sweet inner leaves from a September 1 sowing of 'Dwarf Scotch Curled Kale', the best eating of the traditional kale varieties we have grown under the inner cover. Those plants produced beautiful kale for early-to-mid-March sales before starting to bolt the third week in March. For a spring, summer, and fall kale variety we grow a Tuscan kale exclusively. It goes by the names of 'Toscano', cavalo nero, dinosaur kale, 'Nero di Tuscana', or black kale. Both we and our customers think it is so delicious as to almost transform kale into another vegetable entirely.

## Carrots

"Sweet Winter Carrots" are our most acclaimed winter crop. Parents in nearby towns tell us all the time how much their children like these crunchy treats. We leave these carrots in place in the soil under the cold houses, digging them over time as needed. The most successful variety we have found thus far for wintering in the soil is 'Napoli', a small-size but full-flavor carrot. We plant for October harvest during the last week of July and for later harvests, the first week of August. We plant in soil fertilized by turning under a soil-improving green manure of oats and peas a month before we sow the carrots. We cover large areas of carrots with mobile greenhouses in late October. Our "Sweet Winter Carrots" are always dug fresh from the soil in which they grow; we dig them outdoors in October and November and from the greenhouse-covered beds in December, January, and February. The in-ground, cold-soil storage further enhances their flavor, sweetness, and raw-eating crunch so that the last ones harvested in late February are even sweeter than the first. Since the tops remain green under the inner layer, we sell our carrots with one and one-half inches of green top at all times. This makes for a beautiful pack and identifies our carrots as "freshly harvested" rather than from storage, allowing us to charge a premium price.

These carrots have an almost legendary popularity in our markets. We cannot grow enough of them to meet the demand. The tastiness resulting from fall growing and cool-soil storage elevates the humble carrot to another plane. While delivering in our stores we have seen little children rush to the produce counter, entreating their parents to buy lots of "candy carrots." This crop is at its best for only a five-month season from October through February. Once new top growth begins in March, they start to lose their sweetness.

We have experimented with extending the harvest season of our sweet carrots, but we haven't succeeded yet. We tried adding a layer of insulation over some beds in mid-January to forestall spring regrowth, but that prevented the important daily influx of sun warmth, causing the carrots and the soil to freeze solid for weeks. The carrots were of poor quality when they thawed. We have also planted carrot varieties that resume their root growth in spring from a late-September/early-October sowing date in hopes of finding one that would be harvestable in April. Thus far the flavor has been disappointing.

We sow a new crop of carrots during the winter to sell in the spring. Our new-year sowings of carrots, made in late December following fall lettuce, are ready for sale by May 10. For these we use the variety 'Nelson'. This is a deliciously sweet spring carrot, but no matter how tender and flavorful our spring carrots may be, they cannot match the acclaim of our sweet winter carrots.

## Spinach

If we were to grow only one leafy winter crop, it would be spinach. We sell spinach both as small leaves in the salad mixes and as large leaves for bulk sales. In both cases we harvest only whole leaves without stems. This is slower work than harvesting entire plants, but we continue to do it because it is worth it: the regrowth is much better, which means greater total yield per square foot, and the quality of the product is exceptional enough to command a commensurate price. We harvest with a very sharp small-bladed (bird's-beak) knife and find we have become very efficient with practice.

In our climate spinach planted outdoors during the second to third week of September in well-composted soil and then covered with a greenhouse by late October is ready to harvest for Thanksgiving sales. The plants continue to produce, yielding four more harvests per bed until late March/early April. We devote almost half of our total greenhouse space to winter spinach. For more on spinach, see pages 36 and 126.

## Leeks

Leeks are almost a year-round crop for us and would be all-year if the winter leeks did not sell out so quickly. We get our first crop in May from transplanting extra early seedlings to a cold house. (Seeds are sown February 15 in our plant-starting greenhouse.) Then we sell outdoor-grown summer leeks through September and the fall leeks through November. Winter leeks are available from early December until we are sold out, usually in early March. We use a different leek variety for each season. The summer and fall leeks are harvested directly from the field with the additional protection of a sheet of plastic over the last of the fall leeks during the second half of November. We protect the winter leeks with a movable greenhouse starting in early December. We add an inner layer from mid-December on until all the leeks are sold.

Leeks with long blanched shanks from deep planting.

The edible part of a leek is the white blanched stem. The more length a blanched leek stem has, the better the product. Blanching can be accomplished by hilling soil up against the stems of the leeks. However, in our experience, the key to growing leeks efficiently and intensively is to grow your own transplants and dibble them into deep planting holes. By dibbling in the transplants rather than having to hill-up soil as the leeks grow, we are able to plant them more intensively—as closely as three rows on a 30-inch bed with the leeks 4 inches apart in the row.

Unlike many of our other crops, we don't grow our leek transplants in soil blocks. Instead, we grow them on the floor in our plant-starting greenhouse in 30-inch-wide-by-8-foot-long-by-3-inch-deep seedbeds with wooden sides filled with potting soil. We sow leek seeds directly into these beds using the six-row seeder (see chapter 13). We allow the seedlings to grow in these beds until they are at least 10 inches tall. We dig them out of the seedbed by loosening the potting soil under them with a trowel. To prepare the young plants for transplanting, we trim their roots to 1 inch long and trim the top part to 10 inches long.

Our dibble is a 36-inch-long, 1-inch-diameter dowel with the end tapered to a spatulate tip. We sometimes attach a shovel handle to the upper end of the dowel and add a 6-inch-diameter plate 9 inches above the tip. In use we push it into the soil to the full 9-inch depth and then twist the handle so the spatulate tip flattens out the bottom of a 9-inch-deep tubular hole. This is more successful if the soil is moist, as dry soil will tend to collapse back into the hole when the dibble is removed. Thus, we water the surface before transplanting when conditions are dry. We make a hole every four inches along the row and simply drop a leek transplant vertically into each hole.

Once the seedlings are in the holes, only an inch or so of green top sticks up above the soil. Then we irrigate the field and let the leeks grow. We don't intentionally refill the holes, but soil slowly migrates in every time we irrigate or cultivate. The leek plants grow beautifully, each with a guaranteed nine inches of blanched shank. If you have never grown leeks this way before you may find it hard to believe that it will work—but it does.

Our restaurant customers love early baby leeks. These we grow in a cold greenhouse at five rows to a 30-inch bed, setting them 3 inches apart in the row. At that spacing they can be cultivated with the long-handled wire weeder. Once when we had no other space, we planted single rows of leeks between the edge bed and the wall of the greenhouse. The dibble-and-drop method is the only way we could have done that.

## Mâche

Mâche continues growing right through the winter, no matter how cold the weather. With mâche you harvest and sell the whole plants. We often included mâche in the salad mix during

December, January, and February, its best season. As an ingredient in salad mix, we prefer to cut it at three-quarters of full size.

Since mâche is not a cut-and-come-again crop, properly timed succession sowings are crucial for a steady supply. The late sowings—which allow us to have mâche available all through March—require even more precise timing (i.e., sowing October 25 for harvest on March 1).

If we have an oversupply, we sell full-sized mâche plants in bulk. In Europe mâche was traditionally sold in shallow boxes, one layer deep, with field-grit still clinging. We thoroughly wash our bulk mâche and sell it loose in our standard 3½-pound box.

## Radishes

Demand for our radishes is strong at Thanksgiving and for winter and spring holiday dinners. We succession-plant radishes in the cold houses and have sold them into December from a planting as late as September 30. Radishes are exceptionally mild and crisp in the cold houses in fall and spring but will not grow in winter once continuous freezing temperatures occur. We hope to find a radish cultivar for fall planting that would hold in the soil in excellent condition even after temperatures are too cold for growth.

Radishes can be grown all winter in the cool greenhouse. Radishes are useful as a quick crop in the spring season, and our market demand is stronger in spring than in fall.

## Onions and Scallions

We have purchased onion plants from the Texas growers and set them out in our cool houses the first week in January. We purchased the same short-day varieties that are traditionally grown in Vidalia, Georgia, and our harvest in early May was about the same time as theirs. These varieties produce very large, sweet, round bulbs that were a great hit with local restaurants looking for an early season specialty crop to mention on their menus.

We have also grown winter scallions because they are extremely cold hardy and can even be harvested frozen and recover nicely when they thaw. Unfortunately, Southern growers dump field-grown winter scallions in our markets at prices so low that we often don't bother growing this crop. However, we highly recommend growing overwintered onions such as 'Walla Walla Sweet' and 'Olympic'. We plant seed outdoors in late August and cover with a mobile greenhouse by late November. We sow at five rows per bed. We sell the plants from the two intermediate rows as scallions as soon as they are large enough in spring. We let the other three rows mature into bulbs that are ready for sale five weeks ahead of spring-planted onions. The return on this crop was not always commensurate with the length of time they took up greenhouse space, so we now winter them over under much simpler structures (see chapter 11).

## Watercress

Watercress can be grown like any other salad crop during the winter in the cool and moist conditions of a minimally heated greenhouse. We use boards to frame out 3-inch-tall-by-30-inch-wide beds on the concrete floor of our original cool house. We fill those frames with potting soil and sow twelve rows of watercress from seed. We place small misters (1 gallon per hour output) every 3 feet along the bed and run them continuously. Including watercress in our salad mix gave it an extra level of pizzazz, but we decided it was not cost effective. We get much better return selling watercress as an individual crop.

Watercress growing in 3 inches of potting soil with the aid of misters.

## Beets

We've been successful growing exceptional quality beets and greens in a cold house both late into the fall and very early in spring (we've gotten beets to market six to eight weeks ahead of our outdoor spring crop). For the fall crop, since outdoor field beets can be sold quite late, we have found that a gourmet item like golden beets gives the best return. We choose baby beet varieties for the spring crop because they offer such a refined product when greenhouse grown. We sow them in our plant-starting house three weeks ahead of when we plan to put them in the soil. We sow them as multi-plant blocks (see *The New Organic Grower*, p. 149) at three seeds per block and transplant them out three rows to the bed at 10-inch-by-10-inch spacing.

### MORE MARKETING SAVVY

Swiss chard has long been a popular winter greenhouse crop in France, but we have not found it an easy crop to sell in our markets. We decided that the large chewy leaves and long thick stems may look pretty but were not the most pleasant eating. In an effort to improve that situation we began doing succession plantings of Fordhook chard from which we harvested young, tender leaves, no bigger than your hand and without a stem, as soon as they reached that size. We could take four consecutive cuts before the leaf texture began to toughen. Since the young leaves are so tender and had no tough stem attached we decided a new name would help sales and started selling it as "butter chard." Within two weeks after we intro-

Left-hand leaf is the largest we allow in a baby-leaf salad mix. Right-hand leaf is the largest "butter chard" size.

duced this "new" crop early one spring, half of the restaurants to which we were selling had added a "butter chard" salad to their menus. Such is the power of a little imagination in marketing.

## Potatoes

We devote a considerable area to baby new potatoes in the cold houses each spring. We begin by pre-sprouting the seed potatoes for a month. We start in mid-February by holding the seed potatoes at 70°F for a week in our seed-starting greenhouse to break apical dominance and increase the number of sprouts. We start planting the middle of March. If temperatures threaten to freeze under the inner cover after the potato foliage has emerged we add an extra insulating layer of fabric at night. The first harvest of tender new potatoes is available by about May 10. 'Rose Gold' has proven to be the best variety for this early greenhouse production under our conditions. It is just as early as supposedly earlier varieties we have trialed and much more productive. We plant densely at two

Early planted 'Rose Gold' potatoes at 2 rows per 30-inch bed.

rows to the 30-inch bed (8 to 12 inches apart in the row), and we harvest at golf-ball size.

## Turnips

Our marketing success with turnips and turnip greens has been a pleasant surprise. The variety 'Hakurei' grows such sweet roots and tasty greens under cool conditions and in our well-composted soil that we can never grow enough to meet the demand. We harvest out of doors until late November from beds protected by quick hoops (see chapter 11) and from a cold house up until Christmas. We sow turnips at six rows to the 30-inch bed and thin seedlings to 2 to 3 inches in the row. We cut the greens off and sell them separately from the roots as this keeps both in better condition. You can keep producing turnips all winter in a cool house, but plantings sown from mid-November to mid-December will often go to seed right after the roots reach golf-ball size. You must pay close attention as the plants approach harvest readiness.

Claytonia, one of the hardiest of the winter salad greens, sprouts small flowers in the spring—making it even more beautiful in a salad mix.

## Looking Ahead

Over the years we have branched out past salad into more main-course offerings. Instead of overproducing just one crop like mesclun, for example, and then shipping it to distant markets, we prefer to sell a wider variety of fresh produce to our local markets (ideally no more than a twenty-five-mile radius from the farm). There have been days in the middle of winter when the produce counters of those local stores offered eight different cold-house crops from our farm side by side. We would like to make that twelve or more, and that's why we keep experimenting.

Thanks to the greenhouses we get many of our spring crops to

market three months ahead of the best we could hope to do with outdoor plantings. Our continuing research involves determining precise planting dates and greenhouse space allocation for each crop so as to have as wide a variety of vegetables available continuously from the greenhouses until they begin maturing outdoors. With all of our crops, those we grow now and those we may add in the future, we need to learn what strains are hardier, what strains are less susceptible to bolting, and what strains will germinate in cold soil. We are sure the biology of the vegetable world offers as many solutions as does the technology of floating covers and plastic greenhouses. The most important lesson from all of this is that there are so many possibilities yet to come. We are barely scratching the surface of what the winter harvest is capable of supplying.

It is exciting to think about a future in which the colder states are the source of a large percentage of their own winter vegetables. The northern part of the U.S. may not be able to supply *all* of its fresh winter-vegetable needs from simple protected microclimates, but we sure intend to push the envelope here in Maine. A winter harvest of a wide variety of crops is a logical step for farms that market their produce to subscribers or CSA members. Instead of trying to increase the number of members you serve each year, you could increase the number of months during which you supply food to your current customers.

# chapter nine

# Summer Crops

*From winter, plague and pestilence,*
*good Lord, deliver us.*

—THOMAS NASHE

Many growers who have not tried raising crops in unheated greenhouses are well aware of the value of hothouses for getting warm-weather crops to market well ahead of the usual summer harvest season. Many of them have wondered what crops they might be able to grow in their greenhouses in winter. In our case it was just the opposite. We became involved with greenhouses because of our interest in growing winter crops and then wondered how best to use them for the rest of the year.

Over the course of learning what works best, we have grown crops of sweet potatoes, Charantais melons, salad greens, tomatoes, peppers, eggplants, and cucumbers in our high tunnels during the summer. In addition, we grew arugula, pak choi, and basil in the summer tunnels. Basil, because our summers are cool, and the other two because on our dry, sandy soil it is difficult to grow them free of flea-beetle damage outdoors in the summer, whereas they are not bothered by flea beetles in the greenhouse. We no longer grow melons or sweet potatoes because the economics are in favor of the other crops.

In the early years, when we were concerned with raising the fertility level of our soil, we also grew warm-climate green manures. We were particularly interested in vigorous leguminous crops like black-eyed peas and cowpeas that would benefit from the heat, improve the soil, and yet be totally unrelated to the crops we were growing the rest of the year. The cowpeas were particularly successful, and we found that growing green manures in greenhouses is no different from growing them outdoors (our methods of growing green manures are described in detail in *The New Organic Grower*).

## Getting the Most from Greenhouses in Summer

Using greenhouses to get an earlier start in the spring, during the transition from winter to summer, is a first logical step. Local growers must compete with the "everything all the time" aura of the supermarket. Few customers, even those who prefer to shop at farm stands and farmers markets, understand seasonal realities. So, since simple hoop houses, even without added heat, can mean a four- to twelve-week jump on outdoor maturity (depending on the crop) it makes good business sense to use them fully. In addition, it is worth considering adding heat to a greenhouse (temporarily turning a cold house into a hothouse) to get a real jump on the season for certain must-have crops like tomatoes. Yes, your costs will increase, but the investment is like the loss leader at the supermarket—an item that is sometimes sold almost at cost because it brings in customers who then buy many other items.

We consider three crops—tomatoes, cucumbers, and peppers—to be always worth growing with added heat in order to have them available for sale earlier at our farm stand. Thanks to our unheated hoop houses we do have a surprising number of crops for a farm stand in Maine when we open in early June—arugula, beets and greens, carrots, chard, fennel, herbs, kale, lettuce, pak choi, parsley, potatoes, radishes, scallions, spinach, and turnips, to name a few—but it is the tomato and cucumber signs that catch the public eye. Our aim is to have tomatoes and cucumbers ready when the stand opens and peppers about two to three weeks later. We have experimented with eggplants as a heated crop, but they require far more heat than the crop is worth. Because of our cool coastal climate we grow eggplant in unheated greenhouses even during the summer, transplanting them into the houses at the time of our last frost date.

If you do grow warm-season crops in greenhouses, especially if you add heat at the start, it is definitely worth going to the extra trouble of learning the professional techniques for growing these crops on a vertical support system, because that will more than triple the yield per square foot compared to unsupported crops.

Artichokes attract customers at both farm stands and farmer's markets.

For tomatoes, peppers, and eggplants, these professional techniques, with the addition of monthly topdressing with compost, will extend the lifespan of the plants from early spring, when you set them out, to as late in the fall as you can manage to keep them going.

It's also important to note that there are new variables vis-à-vis crop timing and crop rotation to consider when using greenhouses in both summer and winter. We discuss our approach to these in chapter 10.

## Tomatoes

Tomatoes bring in three times more dollar value than any other single crop at our farm stand. That fact and their customer appeal have encouraged us to put a lot of effort into their care. Outdoor tomatoes don't begin to ripen until early August here on the Maine coast, so a hoop house is a necessity for a farm-stand business. We grow three varieties as basics—an early round red 6- to 10-ounce standard tomato, a later maturing and much larger red beefsteak type, and a cherry tomato for basket sales. Through trials we have sought out and chosen the most flavorful greenhouse-adapted cultivars. The ones that work best for growth, yield, and eating quality on our soil have turned out to be modern varieties. (See appendix D for variety suggestions.) It would be nice to offer our customers a wide selection of heirloom tomatoes as well, but given the constraints of climate and greenhouse space there is not enough room. Our practice and advice to others is to be always on the lookout for better tomato varieties and to run trials with new candidates every year.

**Tomatoes pruned to a single stem.**
Photo by Lynn Karlin.

### Starting Tomato Plants

When raising tomato plants from seed we repot the seedlings twice to ensure uninterrupted root growth. We germinate the seeds in mini-blocks on heat pads at 70°F and move them on to two-inch blocks as soon as we can (seven to eight days). We leave the 2-inch blocks on the heating pads for ten days or so. Before their leaves overlap one another, we put them in their final 5-inch square pots. (This is the only crop for which we use pots because the extra soil volume guarantees sturdy, well-rooted plants.) These pots sit side by side until the leaves begin to touch, and then we start moving them apart. Adequate spacing, so the leaves of one tomato plant don't shade the leaves of another, keeps the plants short. It is much easier to move and transplant younger plants, so we start tomato seeds only six weeks before we plan to set the plants in the greenhouses.

We grow tomatoes using the same system of 30-inch-wide beds with a 12-inch path between them that we use for all other

**A tomato trellis clip secures the stem to the twine.** Photo courtesy of Johnny's Selected Seeds, Winslow, Maine.

crops. There are eight beds in a 30-foot-wide house and the middle six are planted to tomatoes. (For the two edge beds, which do not have enough headspace for staked tomatoes, we have found that both early celery and Tuscan kale transplants grow well and are excellent companion crops in a tomato house.) We set out the tomato plants 24 inches apart down the center of the bed. We could put them closer (down to 14 inches if we had a better native soil) but we enjoy the ease of working with the plants at this wider spacing, not only for the pruning and harvesting but also for the monthly topdressing with compost. The monthly topdressing is very important since, as mentioned earlier, these plants will keep producing until late in the fall. The wider spacing also aids with air circulation, which is important because humidity can be quite high in a plastic-covered hoop house in April.

### Vertical Growing

We support our tomatoes with plastic twine that unrolls from small spools attached to wire frames that hang from horizontal wires running the length of the greenhouse. This is standard equipment in commercial tomato houses. We prune to a single stem by removing all suckers between the leaf branch and the stem. We use commercial tomato trellis clips to secure the tomato stem to the twine, placing a clip about every 12 inches as the plant stem elongates. We limit the fruit clusters on beefsteak varieties to four fruits and those on the medium-sized varieties to five fruits by pruning off the extras. As soon as a cherry tomato cluster begins ripening the first fruit, we pinch off any further blossoms at the end of the cluster.

By the time the plants' growing tips reach the support wire, ideally about 8 feet above the ground, we have harvested the lowest fruit and removed the lower branches up to the height of the lowest fruit cluster. At that point we unroll a turn or two of twine from each spool, lower the top of each plant about 12 inches, and move the tops horizontally by sliding the wire frame that holds the spool along the support wire. At the end of the row, the plants are curved around the corner and over to the partner row that moves horizontally in the other direction. The paired rows resemble those circular trolleys for moving clothes in large dry-cleaning establishments. This dropping of the plant tops and moving them sideways is repeated every time the tops grow to the height of the support wire. The bare stems end up lying along the ground (some growers use low wickets to keep the stems from actually contacting the soil, but we have found no need to do that), and the top 8 feet of each vine keeps producing tomatoes. In this way a crop set out early in the spring stays in vigorous production until late in the fall.

### Managing Timing and Soil Temperature

In our present rotation the largest greenhouse in which we grow tomatoes is occupied all winter by a mid-September-sown unheated spinach crop from which we get four to five harvests before the end of March. We pull the spinach crop in late March/

early April just before it begins to go to seed (later-planted spin-ach in another house allows for uninterrupted production on through the spring) and then immediately refertilize the beds with an inch of compost. We set out the tomato plants on April 7. Since the house has been unheated, we need to warm the soil as much as possible before the tomatoes go in. To do so we pull back the inner covers protecting the spinach every sunny day during March in order to allow more direct solar heating of the soil. Once we remove the spinach plants, we turn on a propane heater for a few days before the tomatoes are transplanted to prevent the night temperatures from falling below 60°F.

In another greenhouse, we clear out the previous crop a month or more before we need the house for tomatoes. We remove the wickets and the row-cover inner layer. We then prepare the soil for the tomato crop and lay a sheet of clear plastic directly on the soil. This is the most effective way to trap incoming solar heat in the soil. It also stimulates weed seed germination, and we flame off the weed seedlings before transplanting the tomatoes (see chapter 14 for more on flaming). By using plastic laid on the soil to create an extra-warm inner layer we have gotten the soil temperature at the 4-inch depth up to 65°F with only solar heat. We cannot get it that warm while continuing to harvest spinach, but we think the income from the spinach more than makes up for the slightly slower start of the tomatoes. These are the sorts of choices the multiple-crop grower must be constantly making.

## Cucumbers

We have tried growing many types of greenhouse cucumbers. We've grown the 14-inch-long lightly ribbed European types (like those usually sold shrink-wrapped in supermarkets) on down to the 3-inch-long seedless baby cucumbers. All have their virtues, but we have learned that our customers prefer a more standard-looking cucumber, about 7 inches long. Fortunately there are a number of varieties adapted to greenhouse culture that fit the bill. It might be nice to offer white or brown or lemon cucumbers in addition, but the demand for what we do grow is so great there is no room left for growing any others.

A greenhouse cucumber, pruned to one stem, trained up over a support bar (7 to 8 feet high) and then back down to the ground, will yield well and remain manageable for about six weeks after it starts producing. This is a heavy-feeding crop demanding the best fertility you can create. Soil preparation for a greenhouse cucumber crop is a no-holds-barred operation. We spread a full inch of our best manure compost and add an organic nitrogen fertilizer in addition. Seaweed is one ingredient in our compost, and we recommend that growers who don't have that resource available use a dried seaweed or commercial trace-element amendment to ensure that trace-element levels in the soil are optimum. If you are starting

Tomatoes, cucumbers, eggplants, and peppers are all pruned and trained vertically in our summer greenhouse production.

with a low organic-matter soil, till in a couple of inches of peat moss with some limestone before you begin cucumber preparation. That will jump-start the increase in soil organic matter.

We sow our greenhouse cucumbers in succession at three-week intervals starting on March 21 and continuing through June 21. We sow in 3-inch soil blocks. These blocks have a ¾-inch cubic indentation at the center. We fill the indentation with fine seed-starting mix and sow one seed per block shallowly into that mix. We germinate them on a heating pad set at 85°F. The seed for greenhouse cucumbers is expensive, and it's important to do everything possible to optimize germination percentage. We transplant seedlings to the greenhouse when they are two weeks old. Some greenhouse cucumber varieties can tolerate night temperatures of 50°F (10°C) but we find that 55° to 60°F (13° to 15°C) gives better establishment and better growth even with a tolerant variety.

Once the plants are in the ground we prune off every sucker and every female flower until the plant is 3 feet tall. At that point the plant has enough roots established to support fruit production. As the plant grows we continue pruning suckers but leave one cucumber at each node on the single stem until the stem is tall enough to go over the support bar. At that point the root system will support even greater production. So right at the top we let one sucker grow in addition to the main stem so as to have two stems per plant trailing over the support bar. We continue to prune out all suckers and leave one cucumber at each node on both vines all the way back down to the ground. Once the cucumbers reach harvest size we pick every day so as to have them at the optimal size. After we harvest the last cucumber at ground level we pull the crop because the younger plantings are more productive and much less work to manage. We replace the pulled crop with celery transplants for fall harvest.

## Peppers and Eggplant

We get the best overall production from peppers if the young plants are transplanted to the greenhouse well before the first flower opens. In the conditions of our plant-starting house that means a plant about seven weeks old. We plan to put them in the soil on May 1. We sow in mini-blocks placed on a heating pad at 80°F and move them to 2-inch blocks and then 5-inch pots, the same as with the tomatoes. We sow eggplants on April 1 so as to have eight-week old transplants by June 1.

We train greenhouse pepper plants vertically as with tomatoes and cucumbers, but in the case of peppers we train to two stems rather than one. We also train eggplants to two stems. In both cases we prune and clip on a weekly schedule, limiting production to one fruit at every node. These techniques are well established, but there are a lot of ingenious people in the greenhouse industry, and new ideas come along all the time. I suggest searching on the Internet every so often to see how techniques for any and all of these crops may have evolved.

## Outdoor Crops

Only one-quarter acre of our acre and a half of vegetable production area is covered with greenhouses, so most of our summer and fall production is in the field. One of the practices we rely upon to get a quick start with early outdoor plantings is to prepare the soil the fall before. In many cases we even prepare the growing beds in the fall so all we have to do in spring is sow seeds or put in transplants. We got into this habit because there always seems to be more time in fall to get work done than in the rush of spring, especially if there is wet spring weather. At first we were conscientious about doing the work as late in the fall as possible so winter freeze-up would prevent any leaching of nutrients. As we began cropping our fields later and later into the fall it became a situation of trying to get the job done after the last harvest rather than waiting to do it at the last moment.

Outdoor salad crops are planted just like those in the greenhouse.

Another unique practice on this farm that adds greatly to our yields is close spacing of all our crops. When we first became greenhouse growers we had to learn to tighten up both in-row and between-row spacing in order to take full advantage of limited greenhouse space. When we had success in the greenhouse with close spacing of crops, such as twelve rows of carrots and six rows of turnips or spinach on a 30-inch-wide bed, we decided to use those spacings in the outdoor fields too, and they work equally well. Much of the credit for high yields from intensive vegetable growing should be given to close spacing and multiple cropping over the course of the year. Put those two practices together with generous applications of compost and early and late cropping and you will have enormous production per acre both in and out of the greenhouses.

# Greenhouse Design

*The disadvantages of gardening under immovable glass structures are fairly obvious. The natural soil . . . can never be exposed to the sweetening influences of the weather. . . .*

—JOHN WEATHERS, *Commercial Gardening* (1913)

The idea of protected cultivation during the colder months has fascinated gardeners since horticulture began. Gardens on south-facing slopes, gardens shielded from cold winter winds by a thick evergreen hedge, or gardens snuggled up against the sunny side of a rock wall to take advantage of the solar heat stored in the rocks are age-old ways of creating protected microclimates. Man's first technological step beyond natural forces, attempting to cover the garden with a translucent layer, can be traced as far back as the time of Pompeii, where thin sheets of mica were used to sheath early greenhouses.

When I first became familiar with greenhouses and saw their incredible potential, I wanted to make them do even more. In order to optimize use I always wanted to get the next crop established before the present crop was finished. Growing transplants wasn't enough: I knew I should be able to find additional methods for increasing the number of harvests per bed per year. The obvious solution was to make the greenhouses movable. If I could establish a winter-harvested crop, say, two months ahead of the time when it would need protection, and leave the warm-season crop growing two months longer, I would actually be getting the equivalent of fourteen months of greenhouse use every twelve months.

I like to refer to the movable greenhouse as "the best new gardening idea of the twenty-first century." Actually, I should say, "rediscovered new idea" since, as I mentioned earlier, the first movable I have a record of (a large expensive glasshouse) was built in England at the end of the nineteenth century. What is new is applying the idea inexpensively to high tunnels. Commercial vegetable growers developed the first movable greenhouse in hopes of a better solution to greenhouse soil-sickness and the consequent build-up of pests and diseases. The options at the time—removing and replacing the soil to a depth of 16 inches or sterilizing with steam—both had their disadvantages in high costs and disruption of soil structure. Then the movable idea fell into disuse as chemicals began to be used to sterilize the soil. We have rediscovered mobile greenhouses because they have enormous potential for today's organic greenhouse growers.

## Size and Strength

We realize now that when we built our first 30-by-96-foot movable houses in 1996, we overengineered them. Never having moved houses of that scale before, we erred on the side of strength. Each rib is reinforced with a crossbar and truss support. Since the houses are 96 feet long and we wanted to ventilate without fans, we equipped them with continuous roof ventilation. Both the extra strength of the trusses and the roof vents were sound decisions and the houses work well, but they cost more than we think is necessary for a winter-harvest greenhouse. Based on that experience we have made different decisions vis-à-vis strength, ventilation, and mobility for new houses erected since.

Our new houses are only 48 feet long by 22 feet wide. Their length was partially dictated by the sites where we built them, but also because we planned on end-wall ventilation. Summer ventilation of a tunnel through the end walls in our climate is adequate as long as the length of the tunnel is no more than three times its width. Too much beyond that ratio and there will be a dead-air spot in the center of the house. A third reason for choosing to build shorter houses was to make them easier to move.

Each hoop of our new houses has a crossbar with a vertical support, but these are nowhere as brawny as the crossbar trusses of the first houses. This lighter construction is supplemented with diagonal braces at each corner of the house. We retained the crossbar on each hoop because we think it is necessary in a mobile house to keep the hoops from splaying when the house is moved. Also, the crossbars provide overhead structure so trellised crops such as tomatoes or cucumbers can be grown in the houses during the summer.

## Making Greenhouses Move

I discussed a number of different options for making greenhouses mobile in *The New Organic Grower*, including a ball-caster design and various skid designs. We have used all of them at one time or another. With our rocky soil it was extremely difficult to drive

A 48-by-22-foot house on 2-by-3-inch galvanized-pipe skids.

A temporary ski tip made of ¼ inch steel on the front of a skid for a sliding greenhouse.

posts for the ball-caster design. Thus, for our second 30-by-96-foot house, we bolted cedar 4×4s as skids to the underside of the angle-iron rail. They make good solid skids, but the resulting skid-to-soil friction is so high that our small tractor is not powerful enough to move the house. So, once a year, we hire the wrecker truck from our local garage (a wonderful, large, two-winch design with extended winch arms) to provide sufficient muscle to move the house. Since we wanted to continue with the skid design and still move the houses with our tractor, we decided on smaller houses and smoother skids.

In our next design the 48-foot-long houses sat on 2-by-3-inch galvanized-pipe skids. The pipes were an off-the-shelf item used as support columns in the gutter-connect models from the same company that sold us the hoop houses. We didn't have to weld uprights to these skids to attach the hoops, as we had to do on the first houses, because the company (see appendix C) also sells a hoop-holding base plate for use when attaching their hoops to concrete foundations. We were able to adapt these base plates for bolting to our skids. We connected three 16-foot lengths of galvanized pipe together to make a skid for a 48-foot greenhouse by milling 2-foot lengths of plastic decking (made from recycled plastic) to fit snugly inside each end of a pipe and then bolting one of the base plates across that seam to hold both pipes together.

When a heavy sled is towed across the ground its front edges tend to sink in, and that's what these movable greenhouses do too. We deal with that in two ways. First, we had a pair of 16-inch-long "ski tips" made out of ¼-inch steel. On moving day,

The view from inside as a greenhouse starts moving. The house will stop just before it reaches the water hydrant and electrical box. The hydrant and electrical box always remain covered by the greenhouse.

we fit these ski tips under the front of the skids. Second, we place a 12-inch-diameter, 12-inch-long section of round log about eight feet in front of each ski. The pulling cables, which are attached to the front of the house, run over the top of the rolling logs to provide some upward force.

We pull with two cables, one on each side of the house. The cables extend straight out in the direction in which the house is to be moved to a pulley attached to a ground anchor at the spot where the house will stop, and then over to the front of the tractor. Since each side of the house is being pulled in a straight line the process goes very easily. When the house is in place it is secured to the ground by bolting the skids at each end to 45-inch-long, 4,000-pound-rated ground anchors that are screwed into the soil.

I have visited a grower in Georgia who took this sled idea and made it simpler and less expensive by fashioning runners out of

**Diagonal supports in rolling greenhouse superstructure.**

lengths of angle iron instead of 2-by-3-inch galvanized pipe. The angle iron lays flat on the soil with the vertical edge on the outside of the greenhouse. The lengths of angle iron are attached, one to the next, with metal plates and bolts, so each runner spans the length of the greenhouse. A pair of holes are drilled every 4 feet into the vertical edge of the angle iron. A greenhouse hoop is placed upright between each pair of holes and bolted solidly to the angle-iron skid with a U-bolt that circles the hoop pipe and is inserted through the two holes and fastened in place. Diagonal braces give stability to the whole structure. It was ingenious and the least expensive sled design I have seen.

Our latest development is a 22-by-48-foot greenhouse on wheels that can be moved by two strong people—no tractor required. For this model we lay lengths of 2-inch-diameter round pipe on the ground under both sides of the greenhouse.

We bolt a metal wheel to the bottom of each leg of the greenhouse hoops. The wheels, which have a curved flange, roll smoothly along the pipes. We used the same wheels as those on gates that roll on the horizontal-pipe crossbars of chain-link fences. Since the hoops of this mobile design receive no vertical support from the rails, we installed extra diagonal supports on the sides as well as in the superstructure. There is also horizontal cross bracing in the upper section of either end so the structure cannot rack as we are moving it.

A length of double wiggle-wire channel (see sidebar) runs along the bottom sides of this greenhouse to provide for attaching the plastic cover. Since this greenhouse sits on wheels there is a small gap between the bottom of the sides (below the wiggle-wire channel) and the ground, and this gap must be closed up in cold weather. To allow for this, when we skin the greenhouse with plastic we leave a 2-foot flange of plastic below the wiggle-wire channel along the bottom of both sides of the house. When a weather-tight seal is needed, we put sandbags in place to hold down the plastic flange (another alternative is to bury the flange in the soil). We fill each bag with 15 pounds of road gravel, which we eventually use to repair roads when the bags deteriorate. Filling the bags with soil dug from the field and later dumping the soil back in the field is another possibility.

The 20-foot-long pipe rails are connected to each other with short lengths of a smaller-diameter pipe that fit inside. Although we move this house to four different sites during the course of a year, at the start we purchased only 100 feet of pipe rail for

The wheels of our pipe rail-and-wheel design for a movable greenhouse.

T-post anchor and homemade attaching bracket for securing the corners of a new rolling greenhouse design.

each side. This was enough to move the house from one site to an adjacent site. If we wished to move the house further, we had to pick up the lengths of pipe the house had rolled off and move them to the other end of the house. We have subsequently purchased the full length of pipe needed (200 feet per side) because we decided it would be easier to have the pipe rails in place for the five or six moves per year that we make with this house. This slightly greater expenditure eliminated what I call the "hassle factor." We have put up with a lot of hassle factor over the years trying to keep costs as low as possible for our different technological innovations. In retrospect I think we often made a lot of extra work for ourselves that it might have been wiser to avoid. It is at least worth thinking about.

Since this house is moved as frequently as once a month and the four sites cover a 200-foot-long area (see plan below), we did not use the screw-in ground anchors described above to secure it in place. Instead, we secure this house at each of the four corners with a metal fence post driven solidly into the ground, at a slight angle to maximize the holding power of the plate at the bottom of the post. We bolt each fence post to a bracket that extends from each corner of the house. Whenever we need to move the house, we can quickly extract these fence posts with a T-post puller. I don't believe the fence-post anchors are quite as secure as the screw-in anchors, but they are very easy to use and we haven't had any problems thus far.

# Ventilation

Once we'd designed the rolling hoop house, simpler ventilation was our next concern. The ridge vents in the larger houses were quite expensive. In most tunnel designs, roll-up sides provide ventilation. The concept is reasonably simple but we rejected it for winter-harvest houses in our climate because snow and ice would hinder the attaching or detaching of the pipe roller and the cold air would infiltrate the greenhouse at soil level, directly at the young plants.

We can envision a roll-up side design that might be successful. The rollable portion of the sidewalls would not extend down to ground level but, rather, would stop 2 or 3 feet above the ground. A separate piece of plastic would cover the lower part of each side of the greenhouse. An opening at that height would remain clear of snow unless very large amounts slid off the roof and accumulated on the ground beside the house. But a drop down side would make even more sense. The higher opening would prevent cold air from coming in directly across the plants.

## WIGGLE WIRE

There are a number of different styles of two-part clamping systems used to quickly attach the plastic cover around the perimeter of a hoop house. One part is bolted or screwed to the greenhouse frame, and the second part fits into the first to lock the plastic sheet in place. I think the simplest of all these styles (and the one I most enjoy working with) consists of a low U-shaped channel into which is inserted a zigzag-shaped length of wire to hold the plastic firmly against the inner surfaces of the channel. Depending on the manufacturer, this product goes by the name of wire-lock or spring lock or poly-lock or wiggle wire. The best designs have a channel deep enough so two or more zigzag wires can be inserted. That is useful either for extra holding power or so the same channel can secure both the end-wall plastic and the top-covering plastic.

### End-Wall Ventilation Design—Sliding Houses

The end-wall design for our 22-by-48-foot sliding houses provides for both high and low ventilation. Each end wall has two 4-foot-wide-by-5-foot-tall access doors side by side in the center of the wall. The base of the doors is 16 inches above ground level. We open the doors for ventilation as needed. There is a permanent crossbar beneath the doors that extends from one side of the greenhouse to the other. The crossbar stiffens the end bows to

Friends help out with an early mobile-greenhouse design.

keep the greenhouse ends from splaying in or out when we move it. We have to step over the crossbar whenever we go in or out of the greenhouse, which is awkward, but it's a fair trade-off for the sturdy end-wall construction.

This design also provides a way to allow additional ventilation in the summer. A strip of plastic covers the space between the crossbar and the soil surface. We roll up the plastic strip when we move the greenhouse over standing crops, and we also open it like a roll-up side during the summer.

### Improved End-Wall Design—Rolling Houses

By placing our most recent mobile-house design on wheels that run on rails, we opened up the possibility of an even better end-wall layout. As noted above, we install a crossbar horizontally across the ends of our sled models to ensure that the skids cannot splay either in or out as we move the house. Since this new house runs on rails, directional stability of the leading edge is assured and we no longer need the crossbar. That change allowed us to design a wide door for easier access and even better ventilation.

Our wheeled houses are constructed with a 12-foot-wide opening at both ends. There is also a narrow (2-foot wide) door for winter access between the large opening and the sidewall. The wide doorway is covered with a piece of plastic secured at the top and sides with wiggle-wire channel. The bottom edge is held down with sandbags. The plastic sheet for the door is attached to a pipe at both top and bottom so it is basically a roll-up (or roll-down) end.

For winter ventilation we unclip the wiggle wire across the top and upper sides of one or both ends and drop the plastic down to open as large an area as required. That way neither snow nor cold air can blow in across the crops at soil level. We close up the opening in the evening. For spring ventilation, once snow is no longer a problem, we roll up the door from the bottom during the day and then down at night just like a roll-up sidewall. In early spring when cold air drafting directly across the crops might be detrimental, we stretch a 2-foot-wide

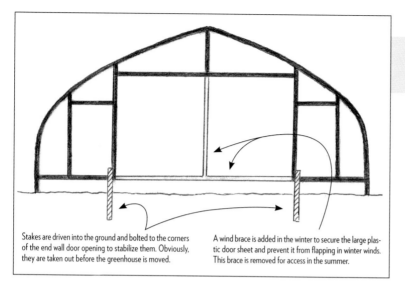

End-wall design for a rolling greenhouse.

Stakes are driven into the ground and bolted to the corners of the end wall door opening to stabilize them. Obviously, they are taken out before the greenhouse is moved.

A wind brace is added in the winter to secure the large plastic door sheet and prevent it from flapping in winter winds. This brace is removed for access in the summer.

piece of plastic horizontally across the bottom of the door as an air barrier (as I suggested for a modified roll-up sidewall system above). When summer arrives, we roll up the doors at both ends entirely and tie them in place. This ensures good ventilation and allows easy access for harvesting or re-preparing the soil for a succession crop.

We are extremely satisfied with our mobile houses and the benefits they offer. Growers who already have greenhouses that don't move will find they can be made to move at a reasonable cost by adding wheels, pipe rails, and diagonal bracing. Or a static house can duplicate some of the benefits of a mobile house if it is uncovered in summer and then re-covered again at the proper time in the fall. The plastic could be rolled up and over starting at one side and left attached to the bottom of the other side. The roll should be covered with an opaque cover to protect it from sunlight. The plastic would then last twice as long without the stress of exposure to the summer sun.

## Designing Rotations with Mobile Greenhouses

Our hope has always been that our small farm could supply the widest possible range of vegetables to our local customers by following a broad-based multiple-crop system for the longest possible season. Our mobile greenhouses have helped us achieve this by allowing us to devise multi-crop and multi-season rotations that we could not otherwise pursue. Here, I'll describe some examples of two-, three-, and four-plot greenhouse rotations with suggestions for appropriate crops.

### Two Plots, One Move

This scenario is the one with which we began and involves a pair of greenhouses, each one moving once during the year, from one plot to an adjoining plot. The two pairs of plots are adjacent to each other, and the two greenhouses are diagonally offset so they don't shade each other. We move the greenhouses in the fall from a summer crop to a winter crop. We usually do this as late in the season as we dare. Our goal is to extend the summer crops' season as long as possible but also to cover the winter salad crops before they suffer any cold damage.

Plot A1 has grown tomatoes sheltered by a greenhouse throughout the summer. On plot A2, which was uncovered during the summer, a summer crop of onions precedes spinach. On Plot B1, a crop of peas preceded winter carrots. Plot B2, was covered by a greenhouse, filled with arugula, pak choi, parsley, and flowers. Both the onions and peas will mature and be harvested early enough to allow sufficient time for soil preparation before the desired sowing dates of the spinach and carrots. We move the houses in the fall so they cover plots A2 and B1 for the winter.

| Plot 1 | | Plot 2 | |
|---|---|---|---|
| A1 | Long-season tomatoes | A2 | Mid-September-sown spinach |
| B1 | August-sown carrots | B2 | Arugula, parsley, flowers, pak choi |

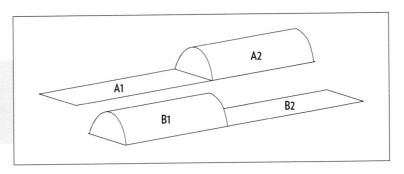

A pair of greenhouses, as described above, after being moved to their winter positions.

When the spinach is finished the following spring on plot A2, we'll prepare the soil yet again and plant tomatoes there. And after the carrots are all dug from plot B1, we plant arugula and its companions there. After that, we'll continue to rotate the crops around the plots, planting tomatoes and spinach in the B plots and carrots, arugula, and companions in the A plots. In this way, the same crop, say tomatoes or carrots, does not return to the same plot but once in four years.

### Three Plots, Three Moves

In mid-October, we move the greenhouse from a summer crop of tomatoes (plot 1) to cover a fall crop of spinach (plot 2) for late November harvest. The house is moved again at the end of November to a third plot to protect leeks for midwinter harvesting. The leeks are hardy enough to deal with the outdoor temperatures until then. As the leeks are sold, each empty bed is re-prepared and sown to carrots starting on February 1. By mid-March when the last of the leeks are gone, the whole house has

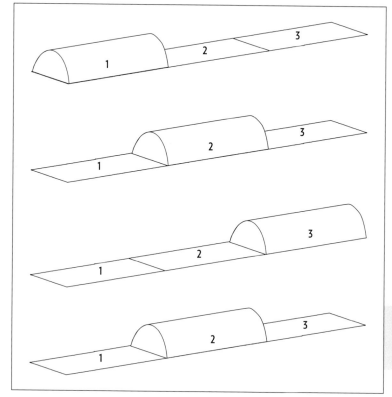

The three-plots, three-moves rotation.

| Plot 1 | Plot 2 | Plot 3 |
|---|---|---|
| Tomatoes in summer | Fall spinach | Leeks followed by carrots |
| Leek transplants | Tomatoes in summer | Carrots followed by lettuce |
| Leeks followed by carrots | Prepared for next year's leeks | Fall spinach |

been planted in early carrots. (By May 1 the carrots no longer need protection, so we move the house back to plot 2, where the spinach grew the previous fall.) In mid-April, we had prepared the soil in this plot for tomatoes and covered it with a sheet of clear plastic to begin warming the soil. We allow a few days for the closed-up greenhouse to continue the soil warming and then set the tomatoes out under the greenhouse around May 5. Around the middle of May back in plot 1, where the tomatoes grew the previous year, we set out the new leek transplants. After harvesting the carrots from plot 3, we plant a summer crop of lettuce, after which we sow spinach in early September and so the cycle is ready to go around again.

## Four Plots, Five Moves

The house spends the winter on plot 1 protecting an overwintered crop that is not hardy enough to survive out of doors in our climate (like late-August-planted onions or late-September-

| Plot 1 | Plot 2 | Plot 3 | Plot 4 |
|---|---|---|---|
| 11/30 to 3/25<br>Overwinter onions | 3/25 to 4/25<br>Early carrots and beets | 4/25 to 5/25<br>Early beans and zucchini | 5/25 to 7/15<br>Summer tomatoes |
| Fall broccoli | 7/15 to 11/30<br>Cucumbers | Zucchini | Tomatoes |
| Ready for carrots, etc. | 7/15 to 11/30<br>Late fall lettuce | 11/30 to 3/25<br>Overwinter onions | |
| 3/25 to 4/25<br>Early carrots and beets | 5/25 to 7/15<br>Summer tomatoes | Overwinter onions | 4/25 to 5/25<br>Early beans and zucchini |

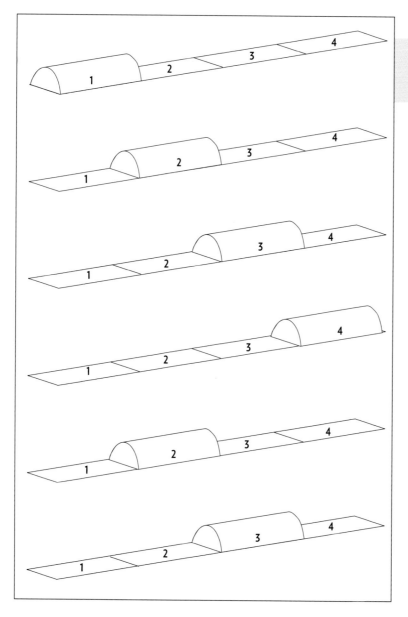

The four-plots, five-moves rotation.

planted spinach). By March 25 the overwintered crop no longer needs protection, and the house is moved to plot 2 to begin warming the soil for an April 1 sowing of carrots and beets. By April 25 the young carrots and beets are safe out of doors, and the house is moved to plot 3 to begin warming the soil for a May 1 transplanting of zucchini and bush beans in alternating beds. Those crops are safe by late May when the house is hauled to plot 4 to cover summer tomatoes. By mid-July the early carrots and beets in plot 2 have been harvested, and the house is moved back there to cover cucumber transplants for a fall harvest. The vertically trained cucumbers will stay productive into October, at which point they are replaced by four-week-old lettuce transplants. Meanwhile a new crop of onions (for overwintering) has been planted in plot 3 in late August following removal of the early zucchini. The onions are hardy enough to remain uncovered until Thanksgiving when the lettuce is harvested, and the house is moved to plot 3 to cover the onions for the winter. Plot 1 is composted and fertilized in late fall so it will be ready for next spring's early carrot and beet sowings on April 1. We also prepare the other uncovered plots in the fall if weather conditions permit.

## Adding Up the Benefits

These examples show that farming with year-round use of greenhouses is a system for generalist producers. Generalists will derive the most benefits from the spatial, temporal, and biological relationships between crops that movable greenhouses help us exploit. (Although a specialist grower who produces at least four or five crops should also benefit by using mobile greenhouses.)

The three-plots, three-moves sequence is based on the progressive hardiness of tomatoes, carrots, and leeks. The four-plots, five-moves sequence is an even finer example of using progressive hardiness of crops to determine the timing and sequence of moving the mobile greenhouse. It also shows the tremendous yields that can result: 1,000 square feet of onions and scallions and the same square footage of early carrots and beets, early zucchini and beans, earlier tomatoes, late-fall cucumbers, and late lettuce—all this from the influence of one 1,000-square-foot greenhouse in one year. That is making very good use of the slight increase in capital investment to purchase a movable house compared to a static house. In addition, many of these crops are harvestable five weeks earlier and/or five weeks later than crops without the greenhouse protection, which increases the length of our sales season by two and a half months.

# chapter eleven

# Year-Round Intensive Cropping

*Work the lazy garden. You pay rent for it all winter, do you not?*
*Make it earn dividends every month of the year.*

—HENRY DREER, *Dreer's Vegetables Under Glass* (1896)

If farmed intensively, a small area of land can be very productive. The key to increased productivity is to make better year-round use of every square foot. The most impressive skill of the old Parisian growers was their ability to develop techniques for maximizing output from their one- to two-acre holdings. When looking to expand production on our own farm, given our limited land base, we refer to finding the "hidden farm." Whenever a section of our land is empty of crops and something could have been growing there, that is the hidden farm.

In our quest to find the hidden farm, the intensity of our cropping has reached the point where we grow almost no green manures anymore because we are growing commercial crops so early and so late. Yes, we lose the organic matter contribution from a green manure, but we gain the organic matter contribution from the root residues, outer leaves, and stems of the harvested crop in addition to the financial return from selling it. We double-crop and triple-crop most of our outdoor fields. We also sow at much closer in-row and between-row spacing than used by large-scale field growers. Not only do we sow twelve rows of baby leaf salads or radishes or carrots on a 30-inch (75 cm) bed in the greenhouses, we use that same close spacing in the field.

Let's take an area on which we plan to grow carrots as an example. We begin outdoor sowings as early in April as we can. Since we try to have every crop available all the time from the moment we first sell it, there are always fields set aside for later sowings of carrots. Some are areas we won't need to sow until June or July. Rather than having those fields in a green manure or cover crop until needed, we use them for early production of unrelated crops, such as lettuce or spinach or Asian greens that can be harvested before the upcoming carrot-sowing date. The same holds true for fields where, say, lettuce will be planted later which are similarly used for an earlier unrelated crop.

Through focusing our planning on double- and triple-cropping, we have achieved gross yields per acre that are almost double what might be expected off our small acreage. Because we sell only in local markets (stores, restaurants, our own farm stand), we need to maintain a consistent production level of everything we grow, which requires even more planning and analysis. If we had a market where we could occasionally come in with large quantities of this or that crop and be able to sell it, we could keep every square foot planted continuously with much less forethought.

We keep harvesting hardy crops from our fields as late in the fall as possible in order to reserve the greenhouse space for even later crops. But we were always wondering if we couldn't do more. In the spirit of Henry Dreer's quotation at the head of this chapter, why should all those fields not covered by cold houses lie unused during the winter months? Given our climate, the only answer to that seemingly ridiculous question would be to build more greenhouses or sow lots of winter green manures. But the expense of a greenhouse is excessive if all we want to do is winter-over hardy crops for early spring harvest. And there are no winter green manures that can be sown and get established in this climate after our late-fall vegetable harvests.

From these musings, we evolved the idea of redesigning low tunnels for winter use. Obviously, crops that are actually harvested during the winter, like leeks, require the easy access of a walk-in tunnel, but we figured that low-growing overwintered crops for extra-early spring harvest would become an economically viable option if protected by a low temporary structure. For inexpensive overwinter protection of fall-planted crops such as onions, spinach, and lettuce, we now use low structures that we call "quick hoops," and we have found them perfect for taking advantage of still more of our "hidden farm."

# Quick Hoops

The supports for our quick hoops are 10-foot lengths of ½-inch electrical conduit, either plastic or metal. Bowed into a half circle, they cover two 30-inch beds side by side with a path between them. We insert each end of the conduit about 10 inches into the soil on either side of the two beds, forming a hoop about 30 inches high at the midpoint. Plastic conduit can be bent as you put each support in place; metal conduit must be pre-bent to the ideal shape with a tubing bender. We place one hoop every 5 feet along the length of the beds (which are usually 50 or 100 feet long). The hoops are then covered initially with 10-foot-wide spun-bonded row cover held down by sandbags placed every 5 feet along the edge (we use the same kind of sandbags as those that hold down the plastic bottom edges of the rolling houses).

Setting the ½-inch plastic electrical conduit for a row of quick hoops.

## Managing Quick Hoops

Onions, scallions, spinach, and lettuce are the first crops we tried overwintering under quick hoops, and we continue to grow these. We plant overwintering onions during the last week of August and place the hoops and the row cover over them in mid-October. As described in chapter 8, we plant onions five rows to a bed so that we can harvest the two intermediate rows as scallions. We start harvesting the scallions as soon as we begin to remove the quick hoops in the spring, which leaves space for the remaining three rows to develop bulbs. The advantage of overwintered onion varieties is that bulbs mature at the end of June. That gives us onions to sell at our stand for five weeks or more before the spring-planted crop is ready.

Three rows of quick hoops cover the same area as a 22-by-48-foot greenhouse at 1/20 the cost.

For spinach and lettuce we either sow directly in the soil or seed in soil blocks. Transplants may be better in some cases because outdoor germination of direct-seeded crops at this time of the fall can be spotty. We seed soil blocks on October 1 and transplant them out two weeks later. Direct-sown seeds would go in at a slightly earlier date. Later sowings will mature later in the spring than earlier sowings, but sowing too late can result in crop failure if the seedlings fail to establish well enough to survive the winter. After setting out the plants we cover them with row cover in mid-October, the same as with the onions. Overwintered lettuce and spinach will give you outdoor crops to sell up to a month earlier than the best you can do with spring transplants. It is important to choose varieties that are hardy enough to put up with the stress of overwintering.

Once real winter weather threatens (late November/early December) we add a sheet of 10-foot-wide clear plastic over the row cover to make the quick-hoop tunnels more snow proof. To stiffen the structure against wind and snow load, it's important to tighten the plastic. We do that by driving a stake into the ground 4 feet from the last hoop at each end of the low tunnel and tying a rope to each end of the plastic. We then pull as tightly as we can on both ends and secure the ropes to the stakes. That makes the plastic cover taut lengthwise. We then shift the sandbags on top of the edges of the plastic to make it taut from side to side. In heavy snow areas, if you are using plastic conduit, you should space the hoops 2½ feet apart.

Using sandbags to secure the edges is much faster and much less work than burying the edges, although it's not as permanent. With sandbags, the covers can blow off in a really strong wind, but once winter arrives and everything freezes to the ground,

## LATE FALL QUICK HOOPS

We also use quick hoops in late fall on a temporary basis to protect outdoor beds of late crops. For example, we now plant even more of our popular August-sown carrots because we know we can harvest them fresh from the cool soil for an additional two weeks. When temperatures below 25°F or an early snowstorm are predicted we can rapidly erect quick hoops and cover them with a layer of clear plastic held down by sand bags. We remove the protection progressively as we harvest the beds.

nothing is going to move. The sandbags also allow us to cover every pair of beds side by side across a field because there is no need to find room to dig a trench and throw the soil aside as one needs to do when burying the edges.

Onions grown from seed sown outdoors in early spring. After the onion harvest, the same land is planted to winter crops before being covered by the greenhouse.

When spring arrives, we start ventilating these structures on sunny days. We remove a few sandbags along the southern edge and insert a notched prop to hold up the edges of the plastic and fabric. Once outdoor temperatures have moderated to the point where the fabric alone is protection enough (late March) we remove the plastic layers and store them until next winter.

## Potential to Explore

Compared to the cost of a movable greenhouse, the economics of using quick hoops over suitable crops are very appealing. Quick hoops can be erected to cover 1,000 square feet (the size of a 22-by-48-foot greenhouse) for only one-twentieth (5 percent) of what it would cost to put up a greenhouse. Furthermore, the quick hoops used for overwintering can be disassembled and moved to cover other crops later in the spring. Quick hoops, because of their simplicity and long season of use, have completely replaced the curved wire wickets that we previously used to support fabric covers over our field crops.

With quick hoops as a low-cost cover, northern growers now have the opportunity to explore late-fall field planting of spring crops, a growing strategy that growers in warmer climates routinely use. However, in expanding this idea, northern growers need to consider these points:

- How early can fall-seeded crops be planted (to have them mature sooner in the spring) without triggering them to go to seed rapidly in the spring?

- At what size and/or stage of growth are young seedlings the hardiest for surviving through cold winter weather?
- What crops can be sown just before the ground freezes (late November/early December in our area) to winter-over as seeds and germinate extra early in the spring?

We conduct trials every winter to try to answer these questions, and we find the third one the most fascinating. Even here in the far north, why shouldn't we sow seeds of peas or carrots or beets or arugula or onions or any number of other hardy crops in late fall for mid-February to mid-March germination? That would put a lot of the remaining hidden farm into production. The seeds might just sit there until conditions began warming in February, but even so, they would be established up to two months before we could get on to the soil for spring planting. We know the concept is sound because we sow carrots during late December in our cold houses and they germinate in a month. According to published tables of seed-germination rates at different temperatures, there are many crops for which this would certainly be possible. We are especially excited by the potential of this practice because we have recorded temperatures as high as 55°F inside the double-covered quick hoops on sunny days in the middle of February. Every day more new ideas for crops and techniques are suggested by what already exists. The winter harvest would appear to have endless potential for all of us involved in exploring it. We are just beginning to tease out the possibilities.

# chapter twelve

# Soil Preparation

*Soil is the tablecloth under the banquet of civilization.*

—STEVEN STOLL, *Larding the Lean Earth* (2002)

Back in the mid-1960s when I was first looking for land to farm, I was fortunate to visit Scott and Helen Nearing. Their book *Living the Good Life* had inspired my interest in organic farming. We became friends, and in 1968 they generously sold me the back part of their farm for the same price they had paid for it twenty years earlier. Since I had very little money, that kindness was truly a gift. However, all the land was wooded with spruce and fir trees, it had very sandy acid soil (pH 4.3), and there were lots of stones left behind by the glacier. Over time we have cleared fourteen of our forty acres, the rest being too wet, too steep, or too seriously rocky to bother with. The larger portion of the cleared land is presently in pasture. But the work involved in turning any of that sandy acid podzol (a soil scientist's term) into high-quality market-garden soil has been another project entirely. With a lot of effort we have removed enough stones and created enough fertility to transform one and one-half acres into a really decent loam. When visitors ask what soil type we are on, I tell them "anthropogenic" (made by human beings). That's one reason I feel kinship with the Parisian growers described in chapter 2, because, as Kropotkin notes, "they make the soil themselves."

When we began serious greenhouse growing, we knew we wanted as perfect a soil as we could create. Most commercial greenhouse vegetable growers grow in artificial media (hydroponics) because they have never learned how to create the ideal greenhouse soil for a natural system.

We knew from experience that we wanted all the soil in the greenhouse to be almost like potting soil, but a potting soil attached to the earth rather than isolated in a flat. We wanted all the benefits that a connection to the living earth confers, such as dependable moisture supply, access for earthworms and other soil creatures, increased depth of rooting, and more. So we spread a 2-inch layer of peat moss over the soil surface (adding enough ground limestone to counteract its acidity) and tilled it in to full tiller-tine depth. Peat moss, which provides very little available plant food, has plenty of slow-to-decompose fibrous organic matter that adds structure to the soil. And good structure, which results in optimum aeration and biological activity, is what all soils need but especially in the semi-artificial confines of the greenhouse. Then the compost, the rock powders, the dried seaweed, the alfalfa meal, or whatever you add subsequently based on the needs of your particular soil, can be fully effective.

Butterhead lettuce thrives in a greenhouse environment.

## Maintaining Fertility

During the initial soil preparation we fertilized the greenhouses with the same minerals—limestone, phosphate rock, and greensand—that are discussed in *The New Organic Grower*. But we have learned that for consistent success, year in and year out, we need to go the next step beyond those basic amendments and focus on rock powders or seaweeds or specific soil minerals to meet the needs of our particular soil. For example, a lot of reading and soil tests and many trials have shown that additional boron is a key supplement for the sandy acid podzol we have been improving. Thus we are engaged in what I would call a deeper organic farming. We pay attention to, and try to optimize, every possible factor affecting the quality of what we grow in order to produce the most nutritious (and pest-free) food possible. (See the discussion in chapter 20.)

Our standard extra-boost fertilizer, between crops in the greenhouse, is alfalfa meal. We like it not only because it works, but

also because it is an amendment we could produce ourselves if necessary. For crops following spinach or claytonia in the winter greenhouse, we have found that some additional nitrogen beyond the alfalfa meal is necessary to make up for the excessive drain on soil reserves by those two heavy-feeding crops. Years ago we used cottonseed meal for that extra boost, but since the advent of GMOs we have shifted to a locally available fertilizer made from dried crab wastes. You can push the crops too hard in the greenhouse using too much high-analysis fertilizer like dried blood, and we are convinced that in most cases and for most crops a "low test" amendment like alfalfa meal is ideal.

Because the beds in our greenhouses are in continuous production of a varying range of crops, soil preparation happens continuously also. The steps involved are clearing away the old crop, aerating the soil, adding amendments, and applying compost. Outdoors we use a ten-horsepower walk-behind rotary tiller for soil preparation, but it would be awkward to use for our frequent replanting of just one or two beds at a time inside the greenhouse. Furthermore, the accumulation of fumes would be noxious. We initially used a human-powered three-tooth cultivator to mix amendments shallowly into the greenhouse beds. It was nicknamed "the human rototiller," and using it was the least popular job on the farm. We wanted a well-designed electric tiller for greenhouse use, but since I could not find one I designed one myself and convinced a local manufacturer to produce it (see appendix C for a source). We named it the "Tilther" since it is designed to work only the top 2 inches of the soil. I decided on 2 inches based on weed research indicating that weed seeds rarely germinate from more than 2 inches deep in the soil. Shallow soil working has always seemed desirable so as not to disturb soil structure, and the 2-inch depth made sense because it would avoid disturbing those dormant weed seeds that were unlikely to germinate as long as we did not move them closer to the soil surface.

The Tilther is designed like a tractor tiller with a chain-drive on the side so it does not leave an untilled gearbox strip in the center. The power comes from a cordless drill that sits on top of

The Tilther is powered by a cordless drill.

The Tilther in action.

the housing and drives a shaft connected by a chain to the tine shaft below. A rope around its trigger is pulled from the handle-bars. This is a wonderfully simple tool with little noise and no fumes. We keep a charger for the cordless drill batteries in the greenhouse.

Before using the Tilther, we aerate the soil by making a pass down the bed with a broadfork. This broadfork has two handles, each 4 feet long, which sit upright at either end of a 30-inch-wide metal crossbar. Seven soil-penetrating tines, each 10 inches long, are attached to the crossbar. The operator applies pressure

The broadfork is used to aerate the soil between succession crops.

with one foot to press the tines into the soil, and then pulls back on the handles just enough to lift and loosen the lower soil slightly. Then the operator raises the tines out of the soil, moves 6 inches further back, and repeats the sequence.

After using the broadfork, we use the Tilther to incorporate any soil amendments needed, such as alfalfa meal, and then we apply compost.

We have learned over the years that compost applications in the greenhouse are most effective when left on the surface, mixed only shallowly into the top ½ inch of the soil. This technique has worked very well, possibly because it mimics Nature where the highest percentage of organic matter is at the surface of the soil. We certainly achieve exceptional germination rates by keeping the compost at the surface. That compost gets turned into the soil at the end of each crop when we go through the process of preparing the soil for the next crop.

We rake the bed smooth and mix in the compost shallowly with a 30-inch-wide Austrian hay rake. One of the wooden-tooth grading rakes sold in many hardware stores is a good second choice. Finally we firm the bed surface lightly with one pass of a 30-inch-wide mesh-surfaced roller. The firming helps to give purchase to the toothed-wheels of the "pinpoint" seeder we use (it's described in the next chapter).

## COMPOST

We spread a layer of our well-finished compost on the soil before each succession crop at the rate of one 5-gallon bucket to each 10 feet of 30-inch-wide bed. If you weigh it out, that comes to a rate of about 15 tons per acre. Since we plant and harvest at least four succession crops per bed in an average year, our yearly compost application works out to about 60 tons per acre. Although that is a lot less than the 100 to 400 tons used by the Parisian growers, it may seem high to some readers. If we had access to unlimited horse-manure supplies as the Parisian growers did we would probably use more ourselves. Soil organic matter, whether from composted manure or composted vegetable wastes, is what powers this system. Intensive growing and intensive harvests mean intensive maintenance of soil fertility. You need high fertility for high production.

## A Four-Season Compost Supply

We make our compost from mowed forage crops with added vegetable wastes and clay as described in *The New Organic Grower*. Since we are close to the rocky Maine coast, we add seaweed. We also add manure produced by our livestock. The compost is turned twice the summer before we begin to use it by loading the compost heap continuously into a small manure spreader that chops, aerates, and throws it out so as to form a windrow as the spreader moves slowly ahead. The end result is a thoroughly decomposed, crumbly product. We spend a lot of time making compost and we use as much as we can make. Good compost is a key ingredient for soil fertility whether in the greenhouse or the open field. Before we got back into livestock, after a fifteen-year hiatus, we would occasionally buy manure compost from a local horse farm. It was made from hay, straw, and manure, but without wood shavings, which I consider detrimental in a vegetable soil. We would limit our purchases to the amount of manure our future livestock would be producing because we wanted to establish the baseline for a truly locally based fertility program for the farm.

In order to have compost available all winter for replanting the greenhouses, we erect a temporary plastic-covered A-frame structure over one of the compost windrows each fall. We build this A-frame out of pieces of straight pipe that are leftover from greenhouse experiments, but it would be just as easy to construct a frame with poles cut from the woods. Wiggle-wire channel up and over each end and sandbags along the bottom hold the plastic on. This structure keeps rain and snow off the compost, protects against leaching, and is sufficient insulation against the cold to prevent more than surface freezing of the ingredients.

A second layer of plastic draped directly over the windrow inside the A-frame is needed from December thru February during really cold winters. In milder winter areas, if you place your windrow in a sunny site and just cover it directly with a sheet of plastic in the late fall held down around the edges with sandbags or rocks, there should always be plenty of thawed compost available.

Structural frame of A-frame greenhouse.
*Inset:* Simple A-frame greenhouse keeps winter compost supply unfrozen.

## Removing Crop Debris

We remove old crops before replanting on a bed-by-bed basis. We always want to get rid of the old plants so as to have a clean seedbed with no decomposing green matter that could inhibit germination of the next crop.

When harvesting heads of lettuce, we remove debris as we harvest, by twisting the plants out of the ground so the fat lower stem is partially removed from the soil. Depending on the baby-leaf salad crop and amount of plant remaining after harvest, we either pull out the old plants, roots and all by hand or, on larger areas, we can clean up faster by mowing off the old crop with a scythe. The technique is actually as much shaving as it is mowing since you want to keep the blade right down along the surface of the soil so as to leave no stubble. I carry a file in my back pocket for frequent re-sharpening of the blade. We collect the green mass with a large lawn rake and place it in baskets to take to the compost heap.

Another way to clean up beds is to use the greens harvester (described in chapter 15) by running the blade along the surface of the soil with a forward motion, so the spent plants fill the cloth basket. Again you will have to re-sharpen the tool frequently. With these techniques, we leave the root mass of the previous crop in the ground, but roots do not have the same inhibitory effect on the germination of the subsequent crop as would incorporated green-leaf residues.

# chapter thirteen

# Sowing

*. . . to plant seeds and watch the renewal of life . . .*

—Charles Dudley Warner

When we began to envision the commercial winter harvest, we looked to Europe to find tools. Our most basic need was a seeder. In order to be economically viable, greenhouse plantings have to be much more intensive than field plantings because space is limited and expensive. Thus, we wanted a multi-row precision seeder for close row spacing. I had put together a homemade model a few years earlier, five Earthway seeders bolted together side by side to plant five rows at 4 inches between the rows (see *New Organic Grower*, p. 73). However, this seeder was a bit awkward to use, and I wanted something smaller and lighter. A lightweight four-row seeder made in Germany turned out to be perfect. Although a simple tool, it was an extremely accurate and precise implement. We named it the "pinpoint seeder."

When it appeared that the German manufacturer might stop production of the pinpoint seeder in 2004, we got together with other interested parties and managed to find a manufacturer who would produce a six-row seeder that contained many features we had found wanting in the pinpoint seeder. (See appendix C for a source.) We still use both seeders, and this chapter describes our experience and recommendations for using them. Most of the information on using the pinpoint seeder applies to using the six-row seeder as well.

We do all our sowing with one of these precision seeders. Three passes with the four-row model will plant up to twelve rows on a 30-inch wide bed (rows 2¼ inches apart). The six-row seeder does it in two passes. The row spacing of 2¼ inches may seem close, but it is common in European greenhouses, not only

A precision seeder, sowing rows at 2 ¼ inches apart, helps make optimal use of greenhouse space.

for baby-leaf salad crops but also radishes at 2 square inches per plant and carrots at 4 square inches. To maximize yields from each square foot of valuable space we sow most of our greenhouse salad and root crops on that 2¼-inch row spacing. Some crops need more space such as spinach, claytonia, and turnips. We plant those at 4½-inch row spacing by filling only every other hopper on the seeder. We credit these precision seeders with practically doubling our yields per square foot over the single-row and homemade multi-row seeders we had used before. These seeders compare very favorably with larger (and ten to fifteen times more expensive) multi-row greenhouse seeders I have seen in Europe.

## The Pinpoint Seeder

This is a tool, not a machine. The difference is that the effectiveness of a tool depends on the care taken by the tool user. The

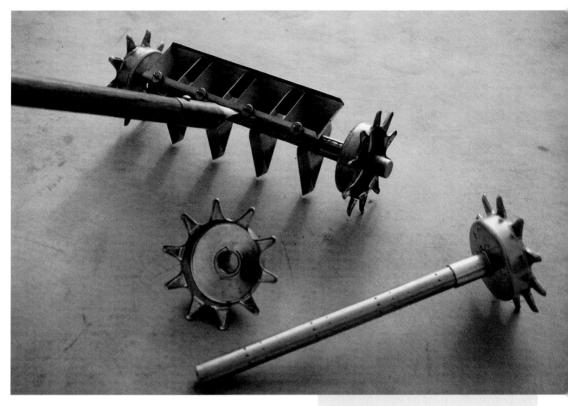

pinpoint seeder uses two seed-selection mecha-
nisms. First, there are four seed-hole sizes on its
movable axle. The axle should be positioned so the desired seed-
hole size is centered under the hoppers. Second, there is a small
brush in each hopper to brush extra seeds out of the seed hole.
Each brush can be adjusted to a tighter or looser setting with a
thumbscrew.

Precision seeders should be used in finely prepared soil. Rocks,
chunks of undecomposed compost, stringy weeds, or root residues will give you fits. The extra production per square foot that
you will gain with precision seeding more than justifies the extra
care in seedbed preparation. For a description of how we prepare
seedbeds, see chapter 12.

The turning of the seeder wheels drives the axle. The pegs on
the wheels give them purchase. However, if the soil is too loose
the wheels can sink in too far and the seeder will bog down
and the axle won't turn. We prevent that by rolling the newly
prepared beds lightly after we rake them smooth. Our preferred

tool for this job is a 30-inch-wide mesh-surfaced roller. The mesh roller does not glaze the soil as a smooth-surface roller would.

The axle of the seeder is held in the desired position by the placement of the wheel shanks. When you slide the wheels into position, leave a slight gap between the wheel shanks and the body of the seeder, so the wheels and axle will turn easily without friction. After years of use, the hubs of my seeder wheels became harder to slide on and off the axle. I carefully filed them out to a larger size and added a hose clamp over each wheel shank. I now snug each wheel in place by tightening the screw on its hose clamp. This is easier to work with than the original friction-fit of the wheels on the axle, and I would now do it right from the start if I bought a new seeder.

Carrots sown at 12 rows to a 30-inch bed.

### Determining Settings

Before sowing any seed, take some time to determine the ideal hole and brush setting. I use the letters A, B, C, D to identify the four hole sizes, with A being the smallest hole and D being the largest. Another letter code, T for tight, M for medium, L for loose, identifies the brush setting. When testing, I fill one hopper and turn the wheel one turn a number of times counting how many seeds drop per turn. The rolling circumference of the wheel is about 9 inches, and there are nine holes for each turn of the axle for sizes A, B, and C, so each of those hole sizes should drop about one seed per inch. Size D has seven holes per rotation. You will want to determine the brush setting based on whether you want a slightly lighter or heavier sowing rate. Subtle adjustments of the brush allow for fine-tuning. For even more flexibility I bought an extra axle and got a machine shop to deepen the seed holes—D by ⅛ inch and A, B, and C by ¹⁄₁₆ inch. The deeper version of hole D now successfully plants the beet and chard seeds that were unsuccessful with the standard axle.

When you decide which hole and which brush setting work best for that particular seed lot, write it on the seed packet. I write my code beginning with the numeral 4 to identify the four-row seeder. For example, I sow most baby-leaf lettuce vari-

| Suggested hole choices for the four-row pinpoint seeder | | | | | | | | | |
|---|---|---|---|---|---|---|---|---|---|
| | A | B | C | D | | A | B | C | D |
| Arugula | | | | | Minutina | | | | |
| Carrot | * | • | | | Radicchio | | | | |
| Claytonia | | | | | Radish | | | | |
| Endive | | | | | Scallion | | | | |
| Lettuce | | | | | Spinach | | | | |
| Mâche | | | | | * naked  • pelleted | | | |

eties at 4BT in the greenhouse and at a slightly higher rate with the brush looser, 4BM, outdoors. I sow arugula at 4AM in the lower light of winter and 4BT in the summer. The table above gives some suggested hole-settings for different crops.

Three of the seeds we sow—claytonia, minutina, and sylvetta—are so small even the smallest hole sows multiple seeds. I set the brushes down tightly when sowing these seeds and have not found the extra seeds problematic since these crops don't seem to mind close growing conditions. I made one modification to the seeder because of these small seeds, however. As the seed hopper was not designed to hold such small seeds, the seeds were falling through the seams. I used liquid solder to carefully fill in all the seams in the seed hoppers. That modification has made a good tool even better.

### Guiding the Seeder

When sowing, I walk backwards down the path next to the bed in order to watch the seeder in operation as I pull it along. If for some reason the wheels are not turning and/or the seeds are not dropping, I want to know immediately so I can fix whatever is amiss. If there is an occasional rock or clump of compost that might knock the seeder off line or gum up the furrow openers, I can stop and remove it.

**The six-row seeder.** Photo courtesy of Johnny's Selected Seeds, Winslow, Maine.

The depth of sowing is adjusted by changing the angle of the handle to the ground. Raising the handle sows seeds more shallowly; lowering the handle sows the seeds more deeply. With practice this becomes second nature, but you need to think about whether a new depth is required each time you change to a different seed.

The furrow openers are designed so the soil falls back quickly following the seed drop. Irrigating after sowing will wash slightly more soil over the seeds if you wish. Or you can tamp the bed lightly with the back of a rake to firm in the seeds. My choice for firming after sowing is the same lightweight mesh roller I use for bed preparation because it also leaves a smooth soil surface, which facilitates the close cutting of mesclun salad crops at harvest.

We use the tooth marks left by the seeder wheels as a guide for lining up the next row. The four-row model is set at 2¼-inch spacing between each row. The wheel tooth marks are 2¼

inches beyond the outside rows. Thus when using the four-row model to sow multiple sets of four rows, the wheel teeth will run directly over a previously sown row if you are spacing the rows evenly. I have never found this to be a problem.

To empty the seeder I tip the seeds from all four hoppers into a 9-inch-wide pan. Then I can pour them back into the seed packet. If you use the seeder with the brushes set down tightly, return them to a loose setting before storing the seeder so they will not become deformed. I store the seeder in a closet at my house to keep it dry and prevent corrosion.

Close-row spacing improves the productivity of the greenhouse.

If the seeder surfaces are wet, seeds will stick. In cold and moist conditions I warm and dry the seeder slightly in front of a heater so that moisture will not condense on its surfaces. One improvement, for really moist conditions when drops of condensed moisture sometimes fall from the greenhouse roof and wet the seeds in the hoppers, is to make a form-fitting Plexiglas cover for the top of the seeder.

## The Six-Row Seeder

Much of the information in the previous section applies here as well. The major difference is that we push this seeder instead of pulling it. In trying to come up with an improved version, we gladly kept those features of the pinpoint seeder that worked well. So the axle with seed holes under the hoppers and the small brushes for adjusting seed flow are very similar. We added a number of features that make this a much more professional tool and one that is usable on larger areas.

- We mounted small mesh rollers in front and behind the seed drop area so we no longer need to make separate passes with our old mesh roller. The front roller levels the soil and the rear roller drives the seed axle and presses the seeds into the soil after they drop. When pushing the tool, it is important to maintain pressure on the rear roller to ensure the seed axle is turning.

- We added three different drive pulleys with a drive belt to allow for delivery of seeds at one per inch, one every two inches, or one every four inches.
- We expanded the size to six rows instead of four so a 30-inch-wide bed can be planted in two passes, one down, and one back.
- We incorporated a seed-depth adjustment into the front roller design so it can be set with a screw knob.

Without the need to roll the bed separately before and after seeding and needing only two rather than three passes to sow a 30-inch bed, the six-row seeder greatly speeds up the process.

# chapter fourteen

# Weed Control

A man of words and not of deeds
is like a garden full of weeds.

—ANONYMOUS

**B**ecause we plant our crops so intensively, we make sure that weeds are under control before our crop seed germinates. Even with crops like baby-leaf salad, which occupy the ground for only a short period of time, too many weeds, such as quick-growing chickweed, can slow harvest dramatically. (Unlike some salad growers, we do not consider chickweed a desirable addition to our baby-leaf salad mix.) The yield increase possible from close spacing on fertile greenhouse soil makes any efforts of the grower toward solving weed problems a worthwhile investment of time.

It is always a better idea to prevent weeds rather than confront them. So our first approach is to see that no weed ever goes to seed. We hand-weed in the fields and greenhouses whenever necessary. We have even hand-weeded green manures to prevent weeds from producing seed, or tilled the green manure under and started again when there were too many weeds. Studies have shown that the serious weed-seed load in a soil can be greatly reduced over three to five years if no new seeds are introduced. However, even under the best of conditions weeds will appear.

## Flaming for Weed Control

Given that reality, our second approach is to dispatch the weeds after they germinate but before the crop appears. The best way to accomplish that goal is with preemergence flaming, which means using a propane flame to kill the weed seedlings on a seeded area just before the crop emerges. The not-yet-emerged crop seeds are insulated from the heat of the flame by the soil. Timing is the key. In practice we like to prepare the area up to two weeks, if possible, before the sowing date, but any length of time is helpful. We will irrigate the area during the pre-sowing time, if necessary, to ensure weed-seed germination. We seed that area without further cultivating, wait the ideal number of days (as explained below), and then flame off the small weeds. This is especially important for the crops planted in rows 2¼ inches apart for which we have never found a cultivating tool that works well.

There are two ways to choose the ideal moment for flaming. In the 1970s we were taught the system used by our European friends who introduced us to flaming. For field crops, they gauged when to flame by using panes of glass about a square foot in size and held about an inch off the ground in a wooden frame. After sowing they placed these randomly on the surface of the field to speed up germination of the crop seeds. They would then flame immediately upon seeing the first crop seed germination under the glass. That works well in early spring, but for summer sowings, when it would get too hot under the glass, we have found it simpler to pay attention and keep notes on days to germination for different crops at different seasons of year and then, leaving a one- or two-day fudge factor, flame off the weeds when the time comes.

When you plant crops in close succession and grow mostly quick-germinating salads, there is not much time for weeds to germinate ahead of the crop, so it's difficult to rely on preemergence flaming with lettuce or arugula. But for the crops that take a while to germinate, like carrots, onions, or parsley, flaming can be effective even if you sow right after preparing the soil; especially against the quick-germinating chickweed, which can be the most troublesome weed in winter greenhouses since it thrives on fertile soils and can both germinate and set seed at surprisingly low temperatures. I have seen a chickweed plant in full bloom in one of our cold houses on January 15.

It is important to remember that flaming involves wilting, not burning the weeds. Experience has shown that exposure to

Experimental flame weeder with cover and roller.

a temperature of 160°F (71°C) for one second is sufficient to melt the protein cells in small weeds (ideally those less than 1 inch tall). The weeds continue to look normal for an hour or two after being flamed, but then wilt and die. Although it may be a satisfying feeling to burn the little buggers to a crisp, keep in mind that burning rather than wilting uses three times as much propane. The design of the flame weeder itself is also helpful in minimizing fuel use.

All of the flamers available for handwork (as opposed to tractor mounted) have burners that I consider way oversized for the job they need to do. Consequently they burn far more propane than is necessary. If the rate of burn is too fast the tank will freeze up (evaporation is a very cooling procedure) and inhibit the flow of propane. The large open flame is also tricky to use near the side of a greenhouse because of the possibility of burning the plastic. The most economical flamer design would have properly sized nozzles for the area to be covered and have a hood over the flame in order to contain the heat. So I have been working on making a flamer with smaller nozzles covered by a hood and a roller behind to maintain optimum height above the soil and take the weight off the operator's arms. A 15-inch-wide model would be very effective on a 30-inch bed with one pass down and back. I haven't perfected it yet, but as I have said before I encourage other growers to design and make tools when the need arises and share the designs to help all of us be more efficient.

## Cultivating

Once weed seedlings appear in the crop, successful control is like the old joke about successful voting in Chicago—do it early and often. I had never found a hoe I liked, so years ago so I designed two models—the "collineal hoe" and the "wire weeder." Both of these hoes are ideal for dispatching small weeds accurately, efficiently, and rapidly. Sharpen the blades, choose the morning of a sunny day, and use these tools, as they are designed to be used, like razors rather than axes. They are perfectly angled to shave small weeds at the surface of the soil. The residues quickly wilt afterward. Shallow hoeing also minimizes any damage to the roots of your crop plants. If rain comes unexpectedly and the cut weeds re-root or another flush of seeds germinates, do it again. Early and often, shallow and efficient, accurate and rapid—with the right tools and the right technique weed control can be consistently successful.

The long-handle wire weeder is very effective if used when weeds are tiny.

The right technique often depends on the weeds. Always try to get to the job before the weeds have grown one inch tall. For small weeds, the technique is to walk in the path between the beds, standing upright and holding the hoe handle with your thumbs pointing up the handle like you would hold a broom to sweep. Always work forwards toward the uncut weeds. Position

the hoe blade about 3 to 6 inches away from you (depending on the size and type of the weed seedlings and their quantity) over the area to be weeded. Then place it on the soil and shave just under the surface back toward you. You can then see if the weeds have all been cut on the area you just passed over. If not do it again. Then move the blade forward another three inches and repeat. (This is somewhat like mowing with a scythe. You move the blade into the uncut area and the motion of the cutting stroke takes the blade back to the cut area.) The return stroke of the blade (moving it back for the next cutting stroke) can be used to further disturb the cut weeds if necessary by keeping the blade in the soil. These are quick motions but since they are short they can be very accurate allowing you to cultivate closely to the stems of the crop plants. Each stroke only takes a second or so. This is a skill that doesn't come naturally to many people (especially doing it with speed and efficiency) so it is worth teaching to your employees.

If the weeds are very tiny and it is a sunny day, you can cultivate a row very rapidly (working in this case in a direction toward the uncut weeds) simply by walking down the path holding the collineal hoe or wire weeder between rows in the bed just slightly under the soil surface. Think of yourself as a tractor and the hoe as one of your cultivators. You can adjust the forward angle of the blade to compensate for slight discrepancies in row spacing. If you keep the depth consistent (never more than ¼ inch) all those tiny weeds will be cut off or ripped out to wilt on the surface. This eliminates the forward/return stroke motion described above, so it takes less time. Always adjust your technique to the size and type of the weeds and the weather conditions.

This idea of adjusting your actions to the conditions is a good example for explaining the greater efficiency shown by a worker familiar with a job. With experience you will find that you are automatically making small efficiency adjustments based on having done it before. How do you become that person? By paying attention while you work no matter what the job. Attention to detail is the major secret to success in any endeavor.

# chapter fifteen

# Harvesting in Winter

*Who loves a garden, still his Eden keeps,*
*Perennial pleasures plants, and wholesome harvests reaps.*

—Amos Bronson Alcott

In the winter, some of the challenges in harvesting crops are different than during the summer. For example, we are often more concerned with keeping our fingers warm than we are about cooling the freshly cut produce. But efficient techniques and good tools remain just as important in winter as in summer.

Our harvest days are Mondays and Thursdays. We deliver our winter crops either late those afternoons or early the following mornings to stores and restaurants in our local area. When harvesting in winter from unheated greenhouses in cold-climate areas, it is often necessary to follow a flexible schedule on harvest days. After a below-zero night we often start late in the unheated houses because we have to wait until the interior air temperature warms above 32°F. Even on the coldest days we can usually count on a harvest window from 10:00 AM until 3:00 PM. Before 10:00 everything is still thawing and after 3:00 it starts to freeze up again. During midwinter having at least one cool greenhouse will pay for itself in efficiency. You can begin harvesting salad crops there in the early morning, then harvest in the cold houses, and return to the cool house to harvest radishes and turnips in late afternoon.

## Staying Warm While Working

In order to be able to guarantee timely delivery to stores and restaurants some supplementary heat may be necessary on occasion. We have a propane-fired salamander heater in reserve for the occasional day when it is so cold and snowy and cloudy that there is not enough sun to warm the unheated houses above freezing. Those days are rare: we have fired up this heater on average only one harvest day each winter. We have never run the heater just to warm ourselves up, but occasionally we have been tempted. On bright sunny days, of course, the harvest window is wider and the temperature inside the houses is downright pleasant.

We dress warmly for harvesting in the cold houses. (I favor a vest instead of a parka.) We cut with small, sharp Victorinox knives (7 inches overall, 3-inch blade) and sharpen them frequently. We place the cut leaves in food-grade five-gallon buckets. If the sun does not warm the houses into the 50°F range, we endure the pain of frosty fingers. We have neoprene gloves available (the ones cold-weather kayakers wear), but I find even the thinnest are awkward to wear while picking. I usually wear one on my knife hand and leave the other hand bare. I soak the bare hand in warm water every time I return to the packing area with full buckets.

**Closely planted mâche is the classic European winter salad crop.**

We've learned from experience to replace the inner covers as soon as we finish harvesting. Once the greenhouse temperatures drop below freezing, the light row-cover material quickly freezes to itself and is impossible to place back over the supporting wickets without tearing. The PVA covers mentioned in chapter 6 are stronger and less of a problem in that regard but, nevertheless, it is still the best practice to re-cover each section as soon as possible.

## Washing and Packing

Since we sell fresh, raw foods we are meticulous about cleanliness. We scrub down the washing and packing area carefully

with hot water after each harvest. All our water comes from a drilled well, and we have that well tested annually. Washing hands is mandatory at all stages of the process. We also wear hats or hairnets while washing and packing. For baby-leaf mixes we wash each of the salad ingredients separately. We have found it easier to spot any bad leaves or occasional detritus when there is only one shape and color of leaf to distinguish them from.

After being washed and spun dry, the individual salad ingredients must be mixed. Our mixer, which looks like a barrel made of wood slats with plywood ends, is 48 inches long and 36 inches in diameter. It is mounted horizontally in a frame so that a handle at one end can turn it. The barrel is divided into two halves, hinged on the long side, so it can be opened like a clamshell. We call it "Pac Man" since it looks like that computer-game character when open. After we have filled the bottom half (it will hold up to 80 pounds) the top half is closed down and latched. Then we turn it ten slow revolutions in each direction, clockwise and counterclockwise. Inside the barrel the ingredients are raised as the side goes up and gently dropped to the bottom again, resulting in a gentle but thorough mixing.

Our homemade salad mixer allows us to wash the baby-leaf salad ingredients separately and then mix them gently afterwards for the finished product.

## Working Efficiently

Originally our labor force consisted of two people—my wife, Barbara, and me. We liked the work because we were producing a high-quality, locally grown product, and we liked working together. We had no intention of making the operation bigger than the two of us could handle. However, we finally gave in to overwhelming demand and expanded production. We now have five employees in summer (fewer in winter) but we insist on maintaining the same high quality standards. In order not to expand the staff further, we are always looking for ways to become more efficient.

We consider and reconsider all aspects of the harvesting, washing, and packing operation. For example, we were able to cut by 75 percent the time required to drain and refill the sinks between washing each of the leaf types of our salad mix by installing larger diameter pipes for both filling and draining the sinks and by raising the water pressure. For the most efficient operation the sinks need to be in continual use. Therefore, we have one person begin washing as soon as the first buckets of salad are harvested. A little analysis always results in a simpler, quicker, and more pleasant way of doing any job.

**Lettuce that is weed free and well grown is easy to harvest and also to sell.**

Coupled with efficiency is speed of work. If you have done a lot of harvesting, you realize that it requires quick hands, a quick mind, and a no-nonsense attitude if you hope to complete harvest on time. The people you hire have to understand that and, if they are talkers, must be able to talk and hustle at the same time. I carefully explain to new employees what the job consists of, the importance of checking for quality and, just as important, the pace at which they need to work. I show them how they should have the harvest container as close as possible to the hand that is holding the harvested item so as to minimize hand travel. I will demonstrate specific skills, such as harvesting spinach leaf by leaf, to show that the more cut leaves they can hold in their hand before dropping them in the container, the more efficient they are. (On average, 40 percent of a harvester's time is spent moving the hand to the container.) I will return a couple of times to quietly reinforce those messages. If they continue to work slowly I will harvest alongside them for a while to see if they notice how much more quickly my container is filling. Some don't notice. I have been tempted to give them one more try by putting their pay on a piece-rate basis to help them understand that this is a business with other expenses involved. I dislike the idea of piecework, but it might be the only way

## STAYING ON TOP OF THE FUTURE

I have used quotes from Andrew Marvell's poem "To His Coy Mistress" for a couple of epigraphs in this book. But there is one additional line from that poem that comes to mind every harvest day and helps keep me focused. I often quote it to our crew. "But at my back I always hear, time's wingéd chariot hurrying near." The next harvest follows quickly after the one you just finished. Since you cannot harvest what you haven't planted, the daily or weekly planting schedule has to be as much a part of your life as is the harvest schedule if you want to succeed. Harvest days and the demands of your customers are just as relentless as "time's wingéd chariot." In this business the products you sell cannot be created instantly but arise from work begun months before. The most important skill you can develop to assure bountiful and timely harvests as a four-season grower is to keep careful notes on seed-to-harvest days throughout the year and prepare from them a day-by-day planting calendar of dates for each crop. Once you can wrap your mind around that reality and learn to follow a rigorous planting schedule, time's chariot will offer nothing but pleasant rides.

to get the message across and/or to suggest, gently, that the work of small farming may not be something they are cut out for.

Even for the most experienced harvesters it is difficult to compete on price while hand-cutting mesclun with knives against the motorized harvesters of the large-scale producers. Thus, in an attempt to make the harvesting of baby-leaf salads more efficient, we have been working with other interested parties on different types of small-scale harvesters. Johnny's Selected Seeds designed and sells a human-powered harvester for baby-leaf salads. Called the Greens Harvester, it consists of a cloth basket collector mounted behind a bow-saw frame that holds a scalloped knife blade. We have designed and are trying to perfect a battery-powered hand harvester for the smaller grower. The ideal tool in our experience would be light enough to use with one hand, easy to carry, adjustable for cutting at different heights above the ground, wide enough to cover one half of a 30-inch (75 cm) bed, and reasonably priced. Small growers would greatly benefit from such a tool, and I am sure that one will eventually appear. I encourage everyone to participate in making this happen.

# chapter sixteen

# SEASONAL SALADS

# Marketing and Economics

*. . . there are many discontents in agriculture which seem to add up to a new vision of "biotic farming." Perhaps the most important of these is the new evidence that poundage or tonnage is no measure of the food-value of farm crops; the products of fertile soil may be qualitatively as well as quantitatively superior. We can bolster poundage from depleted soils by pouring on imported fertility, but we are not necessarily bolstering food-value.*

—ALDO LEOPOLD, A *Sand County Almanac* (1949)

I have been involved in organic agriculture since 1965. In those days the distinctiveness of organic farming gave small growers a unique marketing advantage. Small growers lost that niche when organic became industrialized. Nowadays more and more organic produce is available from faraway sources. Unfortunately, industrial organic produce is nowhere near as well grown or as flavorful as the organic produce from a small family farm. The "profit at all costs" mentality of industrial organics has undermined the traditional values that motivated the organic pioneers. Consequently the word "organic" isn't an adequate distinction anymore. Small farmers need a new way to advertise the superiority of their produce. The important words we have stressed ever since the USDA became involved in organic certification are *fresh* and *local!*

No matter who grew it or how it was grown, produce shipped from faraway is at least a week old by the time it gets to where we live. Long-distance produce is not "fresh" by any definition. Astute eaters, the types who regularly shop at roadside stands and farmers markets, know the superiority of truly fresh vegetables, and they seek out local growers. In order to attract and keep those appreciative food lovers as loyal customers either at our farm stand or in the stores to which we sell, we have focused on establishing a reputation for quality. In addition we have further branded our produce through imaginative packaging.

Beautiful crops and professional presentation are the keys to selling everything you can grow.

## Packaging

We pack for delivery in our own distinctive 12-by-16-by-8-inch wooden boxes, which are homemade from native Maine cedar trees cut on our farm and turned into boards on a neighbor's saw mill. We decided on the reusable box idea years ago after reading that 25 percent of the volume in the average landfill was food-packaging waste. Since we sell only to local markets, it was easy enough for us not to contribute to that waste stream by making our own permanent boxes. Since the store managers approve of the idea, they save and return our boxes to us.

After construction we sand the boxes smooth and coat them with a food-grade finish. Our trademark, "Seasonal Salads," has been burned into the end boards of each box with a branding iron. These boxes look very attractive

**Produce boxed and ready for delivery.**

in produce coolers, catch the customer's eye, establish brand loyalty, and help sell whatever they contain. We determined the size by measuring produce coolers in stores and also measuring the back of our car. At the start, a small business can't afford a separate delivery vehicle. Therefore, we needed to be able to put up to forty-eight boxes in the back of our Subaru for delivering. Once the business grew to the point where we had to make two or three trips each delivery day, we purchased a used van.

Before being filled, the boxes are lined with a sheet of pure cellophane that folds over the top of the ingredients and is held in place by two rubber bands. We chose cellophane over plastic because it is made from wood fibers. That seemed a more appropriate choice than plastic since wood is one of the products of our farm. We also appreciated the fact that this is pure cellophane, which can be composted for disposal after use. Each time we deliver produce to our customers, we pick up the empty boxes from the previous delivery. Back at the farm, we clean the boxes with hot water and store them for the next harvest.

## Setting Prices

Before we walked into stores and restaurants in October 1995 with our first commercial winter-harvest crops to sell, we calculated the wholesale price we needed to receive in order to make a "fair" return. Our price was $2 per pound higher than the price that week for California organic salad mixes, but we were confident in our product's superior quality. The local food co-op took a few boxes for trial and set ours side by side with the West Coast competition. A day later ours had all sold and the competition was still sitting there. The co-op realized that customers were willing to pay more for our obviously fresher product. Chefs immediately recognized the quality and the marketing cachet of serving a "local" salad, and they were further gratified by the freshness of our mix since the week-old imported product they were buying had a short shelf life after delivery. In one local store, where they had never carried our sort of products

## HEALTH ASSURANCE

We have often suggested that the average American spending hundreds of dollars a month on *sickness insurance* would be wiser to invest in *health assurance* by spending an additional $10 per day on high quality local fruits and vegetables. That would increase the market enormously for local growers and benefit their customers an equal amount. The two areas of human activity that we consider most important to the well-being of the human species—nourishing bodies with exceptional food and nourishing minds with exceptional schools—are two of the most neglected and underpaid in our culture. We will continue to make the case that quality produce and quality people are worth a "good" price.

before, the quality of our salad and other vegetables *created* a market. For their convenience we pack the salad in quarter-pound bags as opposed to bulk boxes. That account has now expanded to eight times the initial quantities.

When it comes to food prices, "fair" has two different meanings— "affordable" and "equitable." The most difficult challenge for the small-scale grower producing high-quality vegetable crops is charging an equitable price—sufficient to make a decent living—without being accused of being elitist or unfair. Even though most people can easily discern the quality difference between brands of automobiles or appliances, that same astuteness, with the exception of visible cosmetic quality, does not seem to be applied to vegetables. The myth has been successfully planted in the public mind (possibly for the benefit of homogeneous supermarkets) that *biological* quality differences do not exist and a carrot is a carrot is a carrot.

That myth is patently untrue. In forty years of growing crops and feeding livestock and people I have seen many striking examples of superior biological quality in properly grown crops. There is as much quality difference between our carrots and run-of-the-mill supermarket carrots as there is between a Volvo and a Corvair. And there is a similar difference between local "organic" and imported "organic." The small-scale local

Young 'Bianca Riccia' endive.

Our farm stand with perennial flowerbeds in front.

grower can produce a more finely crafted product through meticulous attention to soil care, superior compost, and variety selection than can the large-scale ship-per. Add the obvious benefits of fresh over week old (we deliver within twelve to twenty-four hours after harvest), and there is no question: the dedicated local grower is selling a premium product and deserves a premium price commensurate with that quality.

Higher food quality is a plus in marketing both for us and for the stores that retail our produce. Every day more articles are published in peer-reviewed journals attesting to the nutri-tional superiority of food raised with organic and other natural techniques. According to studies on levels of antioxidants in vegetables, the winter harvest would seem to offer an additional benefit. Highly colored foods grown under cool conditions have been shown to be much higher in anthocyanins, one of the most valuable antioxidants. One example where this can be easily noticed is in the much deeper red color of red lettuces and 'Bull's

Blood' beet leaves from the winter greenhouse. Green leaves can also be high in anthocyanins since they utilize them to resist cold. It will be interesting to note what future research determines about the enhanced nutritional quality of cold-weather crops.

## Making It Pay

When we began commercial winter production, we set a target return per square foot for our 12,000 square feet of greenhouse space in order to create an economic guideline for ourselves. We figured on getting three crops per year from each square foot of unheated production and set a target of $5 per square foot for the year. This is about one-third of the expected return per square foot in large heated commercial greenhouses growing flowers. That seemed reasonable since we did not have heating expenses and we

One year, when we had extra outdoor carrots in late fall, these "Thanksgiving Gift Packs" helped us triple sales.

were growing vegetables rather than the more pricey flowers. In the cool houses we figured on six crops per year and aimed for a $10-per-square-foot yearly return. Thus it was obvious that each crop had to return just over $1.50 per square foot. Those computations have been very useful in helping us to judge which crops are paying their way.

At the start we knew we were entering unknown realms with our winter harvest and had a lot to learn, so we gave ourselves five years to reach the target gross. In the early years we made all the mistakes this book is attempting to spare others from making—poor timing of plantings, poor choice of cultivar, inadequate knowledge of regrowth characteristics, plus many square feet devoted to trial crops that didn't work out and were never salable. All of those limited our returns. Still, increase in income has been steady and we have achieved a gross return from both field crops and greenhouse crops together of $80,000 per acre per year. Impressive as that may sound, keep in mind that it is not gross income but net income that makes a living for the farmer. Much of our present effort in trying to develop new tools is an attempt to make our operations ever more efficient and improve the net by cutting down on labor costs.

# chapter seventeen

# Pests

Consider the little mouse, how sagacious an animal it is which
never entrusts its life to one hole only.

—Titus Macius Plautus

We have often joked that our worst pests in the winter harvest are our devoted customers who pester us on those occasions when our supply is unable to meet their demand. It may
not be quite that perfect, but pests in the form of insects and
diseases have not been a real consideration, and we have found
little new to report since I discussed this topic in *The New Organic Grower*. The major pest that has developed is not a bug or
a microbe but a mammal. We are engaged in a battle of wits with
the meadow vole.

Meadow voles (*Microtus pennsylvanicus*) look like chubby,
extra-furry mice. All of their qualities make them difficult to
control on the small farm:

- They live out of doors.
- They are serious pests for the fruit-tree grower as well
  as for us because they girdle the bark of young trees.
- They are vegetarians and seem to like our crops as
  much as our customers do.
- They need to eat their weight in plant food every day
  because their metabolism is so high.
- They can breed at thirty-five to forty days old, they
  can breed year-round, and they can have up to ten
  litters a year with three to six young each time.
- They tunnel under the soil and thus into the
  greenhouse.
- They live in underground burrows, and they like to
  line their nests with chewed-up shreds of row-cover
  fabric.

Not surprisingly, they consider our greenhouses an idyllic place to spend the winter.

## Imperfect Prevention

Our first response to any problem is prevention rather than cure. That would seem to be the obvious course of action in this case. However, the mobile-greenhouse concept makes prevention more difficult. We have tried mobile-greenhouse designs with more deeply buried edges to keep voles from burrowing under. We have worked diligently to block any and all small holes that might allow vole ingress. But even after we have taken all precautions, the forces created by winter freezing and thawing can open new holes. In short, we have not been successful at keeping them out. In many cases they are already surreptitiously established before we even move the houses to their winter sites.

Although I am a mild-mannered sort and show great kindness and respect to wild creatures in general, I admit to a strong aversion to voles in the winter greenhouse. My efforts are not yet quite as manic as those of Bill Murray in *Caddyshack*, but I notice a fleeting resemblance on occasions. I have considered any and all options short of bombs, poisons, or chemicals. At present, I rely on snap traps and I use a lot of them. I know from my records that one year I trapped over fifty voles in the vicinity of the greenhouses during August and September, and a neighbor's cat probably got almost that many. Come winter it didn't seem as if we had even made a dent. The only effective method we've found is to keep trapping year-round.

## Trapping Techniques

The usual rat and mouse baits like cheese don't work for these fruit and vegetable eaters. Besides, there is just too much delicious food available in the greenhouses. In addition to the recom-

mended slices of raw fruit, we found a few other baits that often produced good initial results. We even baited some of our traps with wild-strawberry flavored bubble gum. Whatever devious ingenuity went into concocting that flavor to tempt little children, it appeared effective at tempting voles in midwinter when fruit has been scarce in the vole diet. Macadamia-nut butter from the health food store seemed to work better than peanut butter. Then we added carob powder to the macadamia-nut butter and that was momentarily successful. But we eventually realized the flaw with all baits and why we had to keep changing

## VOLE PREDATORS

Many wild predators consider voles little furry snacks and we make every effort to help them find dinner. We keep the grass mowed very closely around fields and greenhouses so that foxes, coyotes, skunks, and owls and other raptors can easily spot the scurrying vole. According to wildlife studies, a pair of barn owls with chicks will dispatch up to 3,000 rodents in one breeding season. Owl nest boxes and raptor perches are useful additions to the farm landscape. Foxes, coyotes, and bobcats can be effective vole deterrents even if they never come around the farm. Scent pellets containing urine from these predators are available, and fear alone will effectively keep voles from entering a scented area. See appendix C.

them. The voles became wise to what we were doing. We could imagine the third vole that approached a baited trap thinking, "Uh-oh, the last time I smelled that Uncle Harry bought the farm," and shying away. We then learned to place the traps so as to intercept the voles' lines of travel. That meant, for example, at the entrances to their burrows, across the surface runs they use when moving from one burrow to another, and up against walls, since they like to scurry along edges. When successful, these traps seemed to catch voles simply because of accurate placement.

Based on that experience our next strategic development was to do away with baits completely and take advantage of another common vole behavior—the tendency to enter small dark holes. This was the key to success. We built wooden boxes about 12 inches long, 8 inches wide, and 6 inches deep with a bottom attached but with a removable top. At one corner of each of the 8-inch ends we drilled a rough mouse-sized hole at floor level. We place an un-baited trap inside each entrance hole. When voles do what voles do, darting into small dark holes, the traps get them. After the first vole enters the box it smells like vole and they seem to have no aversion to it. Every morning we lift the top, empty the traps, and reset them. This solution has been, and continues to be, impressively effective.

# chapter eighteen

# Insects and Diseases

*The art of land doctoring is being practiced with vigor, but the science of land health is yet to be born.*

— ALDO LEOPOLD, *A Sand County Almanac* (1949)

**B**oth of my previous books include a chapter in which I explain my nonconfrontational philosophy about insect pests and plant diseases. I feel obliged to write yet again about this topic because I believe the subject is crucial to understanding the potential of successful human interaction with the natural world through a biologically based agriculture. The organic grower who does not understand the importance of cause correction rather than symptom treatment in preventing insect and disease problems is missing out on the pest philosophy of the future.

This book focuses much more on greenhouse growing than my previous books do, and you may be wondering whether that affects how I apply my philosophy. Once we add the artificial confines of a greenhouse, aren't we just asking for trouble? I do not believe so. What I do believe is that a successful partnership with the natural world requires a complete overhauling of our attitude toward pests. Let me lay it out for you.

Bug picking is not the answer. It is just a temporary solution. The same goes for garlic spray, red pepper, herbal concoctions, necromancy, or whatever. Nor, obviously, are DDT, Malathion, Parathion, Tepp, Rotenone, Sevin, Lindane, Pyrethrum, or any of the thousands of unpronounceable horrors in the lexicon of the agricultural chemist. Basically, none of these techniques, whether chemical or "organic," is any different from the others. They are all palliatives. The word *palliative*, derived from the Latin *pallium*, a cloak, is defined as an action that lessens the pain or masks the symptoms of a problem without curing it. To use a palliative is to cloak or hide the problem.

Insects and disease are not the problem. They are, rather, the symptoms. Their presence is a visible exterior indication that all is not well with the plants. No one would be so simple as to think that scraping off the spots—the visible exterior symptoms—could cure a child's chicken pox. Similarly, removing pests from a plant does not cure the problem or eliminate the cause. All that it accomplishes is to throw a cloak over the problem.

From a commonsense point of view the organic farmer is to be praised for the decision to avoid toxic chemicals. However, from the point of view of creating a long-term dependable agriculture, the organic farmer who uses natural insecticides is no wiser than his chemical counterpart; different materials but the same mistake.

A field of healthy crops about to be covered by a movable greenhouse.

## The First Rule

Once you become determined to eliminate the cause of insects and disease rather than just mask the symptoms, a whole new world opens up. A plant bothered by pest or disease need no longer be seen in the negative. The plant can now be looked upon as your coworker. It is communicating with you. It is saying that conditions are not conducive to its optimum growth and that if the plants are to be healthier next year, the soil must be improved. But to succeed at that you have to accept what I call the first rule of biological agriculture—"Nature makes sense." If something is not working, it is the farmer's, not Nature's, fault. The farmer has made the mistake. You have to have faith in the rational design of the natural world, and thus have an expectation of success, if you hope to understand the potential for succeeding. To do so, it helps to restate Darwin more correctly as "the un-survival of the unfit."

So how do you learn to grow "fit" plants? By asking yourself a lot of questions:

- Is the soil ready for that crop, or should the rotation or choice of cultural practices be changed? (Some, like the Brassicae, benefit from higher nitrogen availability; others, like tomatoes, will produce all leaves and no fruit when given extra nitrogen.)
- How long ago were the green manure or the crop residues turned under? (Three weeks is the minimum. The soil bacteria need time to digest the green matter and return the soil to its balanced state.)
- Was the compost mature? (Testing kits are available. Immature compost can cause a wide range of problems.)
- What was the preceding crop? (If it was a heavy feeder, are more nutrients necessary?)
- Have you corrected the mineral deficiencies indicated by your soil test? (Trace elements can often be the key. You need a complete soil analysis to get that information.)
- Were the transplants stressed? (If transplanting on a dry, windy day, you need to irrigate immediately. Crops like melons, squash, and cucumbers, for example, which must be transplanted with care, will be far more resistant to cucumber beetles if you give them a few weeks protection by a lightweight spun-bonded cover until they recover from transplant stress.)
- Have you chisel-plowed or subsoiled to break up the hardpan? (Impenetrable or airless conditions under the surface are invisible until you plant a crop and then wonder why it is having problems. Take a shovel and do some digging to find out.)

The idea of learning from your plants that something is amiss and needs correcting is nothing new. Any textbook on mineral deficiency in plants will contain pictures of the symptoms exhibited by plants in response to various mineral deficiencies. A common example that many growers have probably noted is the yellowing of corn leaves when insufficient nitrogen is available.

The appearance of insects or disease is just as certain an indication of inadequate growing conditions as are yellowed leaves. The remedy is the same: improve the growing conditions by figuring out what is missing. To accomplish that one must learn what soil conditions favor optimum growth and then attempt to achieve them.

## Learn by Observing

Take your lawn as an example. Say you have a lawn that is growing mostly crab grass, sorrel, dandelions, and other weeds but none of the finer grasses that you would prefer. There are two courses of action. For one you could purchase all the heavily advertised nostrums, herbicides, fertilizers, and stimulants to suppress the weed competition so the finer grasses would be able to struggle ahead. Conversely, you could study the optimum growing conditions for the grasses you want and then by adding compost, rock powders, peat moss, manure, aerating, draining, or whatever seemed indicated, you could try to create the soil conditions under which the finer grasses thrive. If you doubt this approach, look closely at wild vegetation on undisturbed land. Certain groups and types of plants grow in one place and not another. The native vegetation is an excellent indication of how differing soil conditions favor the physiological needs of some plants over others.

The same approach suggested for the lawn is valid on the market garden. Whatever crop you want to grow, you need to strive to create the ideal conditions for its needs. Determining the conditions at first may require a little detective work. Closely observe the plants, the insects, the diseases, and every aspect of the garden. Are all the plants equally affected or are those at one end of the row or along one edge not showing symptoms? What is the difference in the soil of those areas? Is that where you limed or didn't lime because you ran out? Did you compost that area with compost from a different windrow? Did you chisel-plow the whole field or just along that edge? Is the good section

'Indigo' radicchio.

where all the fall leaves end up being blown onto? Or where that old pile of rotten hay bales sat for years? If you can find no clues to follow use different soil-building techniques in general next year. Use different types of organic matter or rock powders or trace elements. Make and use more compost. Change your crop rotation. Organize and evaluate all the possibilities and keep experimenting.

## An Aphidian Example

The one plant pest we have noted in the winter greenhouse is aphids, which appear on our spinach starting in early to mid February. At first, we didn't mind a few aphids since they washed off easily when we cleaned the spinach. But then aphid predators appeared, and the carcasses of the aphids they had preyed upon stuck to the back of the leaves. When we researched the conditions that cause aphids to flourish, all the literature mentioned nitrogen levels in the soil as the main factor in aphid multiplication. We knew that nitrogen could build up in the soil when there has been no rain or irrigation to flush it. Up till then we had traditionally not watered in the greenhouses from about mid-November to early March since the soil seemed moist enough and evaporation levels were low along with the low sun angle. That seemed simple enough to correct. So the following year we began irrigating thoroughly once a week on sunny mornings starting in mid-January to flush out the excess nitrogen and our aphid problem went away. The extra moisture did not cause any new problems and we continue the practice to the present day.

## The Ideal of Organic Farming

Lady Eve Balfour, the British organic pioneer, wrote eloquently about how the early organic farmers solved problems successfully by combining imagination with a belief that answers exist if one looks for them:

> Without understanding all that is, or may be, involved, it would appear that by his insistence on the importance of life; of the return of all organic wastes to the soil; of a diversity of crops and livestock; of the right to existence of fauna and flora other than those of direct economic value to himself; by his avoidance of crude chemicals, and his attempt to provide the conditions in which natural biological balance will prevent the multiplication of any one species to pest proportions, the organic cultivator has evolved practices which will one day be recognized as far more scientific than those which at present pass under that name. Many of the so-called improvements in modern agricultural techniques have been well described by Aldo Leopold as improvements to the pump—not to the well. They have been developed as the result of

a process of thought which has ignored the complex interplay of species which built the original fertile soils; which has deliberately planned the destruction of whole species without a thought being given as to whether their continued existence may be necessary to maintenance of the soil fertility they helped to build; which has advocated remedial measures, to deal with the problems arising from a declining fertility, which treat symptoms only, and which, ignoring nature's danger signals, "protect" plants, weakened to the point of having already lost their capacity for "internal self-renewal," with death-dealing sprays. Thus, to food which is already low in nutritional value (the capacity to transmit energy) is now added the hazard of a host of poisons.

Palliatives are the easy way. But they don't solve the problem. Whereas momentary reliance on them is understandable, they should never form the basis of your agricultural practices. Removing the symptoms may seem to improve the situation but it is only a cosmetic improvement. Working to establish optimum soil conditions is the most constructive approach in a dependable long-range philosophy of agriculture.

# chapter nineteen

# Tools for the Small Farm

*Tools were made, and born were hands,*
*Every farmer understands.*

— WILLIAM BLAKE

One of my first experiences as a garden-tool "expert" many years ago was a classic comeuppance. I had been hired as a consultant on rural food production. I was demonstrating a tool that I had anointed the "ideal planting hoe" to a group of listeners in a small community garden. An older woman on the edge of the group, after observing my efforts said, "Shucks, I got better than that," and strode off to the tool shed. She came back carrying an ancient broom with short, worn bristles. Holding it upside down she used the tip of the wooden handle to make a neat furrow in the soil and dropped in a row of bean seeds. Turning the broom right side up, she then deftly brushed soil to cover the seeds and firmed it with the worn bristles. Enough said. I had learned a lesson about tools that has served me well since. Everyone who grows plants has a favorite tool, and given the number of and ingenuity of gardeners, there is no end to the many simple solutions for making almost any garden task easier.

Garden tools work best as an extension of the gardener's wishes. They should help translate intention into action. However, many people have not had the experience and familiarity with tools that would give them confidence to think they might know better than the experts. Too often, when we purchase what is essentially someone else's design, we assume it is correct. If a tool seems awkward to work with, many people will assume it is their fault because they don't know how to use it well. That may be true occasionally but more likely the tool was not designed to do what your sense of the job wants it to do.

If you think about that old broom, it was truly a wonderful invention. First, it was inexpensive because it had been recycled. Second, it did more than one job (it furrowed, covered, and firmed) with no moving parts. Third, it saved bending or kneeling since it could be used in a standing position. And, fourth, those short stiff bristles would also be effective at cultivating out small weeds. (Tractor-scale brush hoes have been popular in commercial vegetable growing.) Finally, it obviously fulfilled its innovator's sense of the job she wished to do and gave her delight because of its simplicity and effectiveness.

## Finding Good Tools

The garden tools in a hardware store are mass-market items. The shapes and sizes available are limited in order to minimize costs and maximize profits—ease of use is not the goal. Years ago when farm and garden tools were used by professionals as well as by amateurs, the choices were far broader and tool designs were based on efficient use rather than marketing. A look through old tool catalogs or the collection in a historical museum will give you some idea. Nuances abounded. Shovel catalogs offered all conceivable blade sizes, shapes, and angles. Regional peculiarities were acknowledged. I have an old tool book with pictures of dozens of English hedging knives (billhooks). Each slight variation in design is named after the town or county where it evolved. They were the distillation of centuries of local experience in cutting the different varieties of hedge plants common to different climates and different soils.

This functional diversity still exists on small farms in Europe. For example, over many years I have taken photos of different styles of wheelbarrow. Whether single or double wheeled, wide or narrow, decked or open, there was no single perfect design, but rather many aspirations to perfection. In addition, the farmers had added cuts or bends or welds to the standard models to fit them even more precisely to their needs. It was like looking at an author's drafts or an artist's sketches—a study in the creation and evolution of an idea.

Those who engage in sports encounter similar distinctions and

refinements every day. Enormous amounts of time, money, thought, and ingenuity go into perfecting sports "tools" such as golf clubs, tennis rackets, and skis. Think what a difference graphite shafts, larger sweet spots, and metal laminates have made. How often in your farming endeavors have you wondered whether things would work better if the equipment were modified in a certain way. Although there seems to be an appreciation for quality workmanship in farm and garden tools there does not seem to be a market for the nuances of perfection as in sports. The answer to that is to be your own innovator.

The bricklayer's trowel on the right has been modified into the transplant trowel on the left by cutting off the tip of the blade and lowering the angle of the handle.

Modifying existing tools or inventing your own is not complicated. Inventing doesn't have to mean factories and engineering degrees, just imagination and ingenuity. Creativity means escaping from the traditional patterns in order to see things differently. You can accomplish wonders with a hacksaw, a file, a drill, a pair of pliers, and a vise. Stop considering the tool you have as a finished product rather, consider it as a point of departure.

A good example was our desire, years ago, to improve the hoes on our farm. Although most hoes we owned had a large blade at

Different tools, requiring different hand positions. The result is wrist strain with the conventional trowel but not with the modified bricklayer's trowel.

a 90-degree angle to the handle, there were a few with smaller blades at an 80-degree angle, and they were somewhat more pleasant to use. Off to the workbench we went with a couple of sacrificial hoes and proceeded to cut, bend, and file. After repeated trips back to the fields to try them out we came up with a prototype with a narrow blade (7 inches side to side and 1 inch front to back) and with the neck bent to hold the cutting edge of the blade in line with the handle at a 75-degree angle.

After further experimentation with many eager participants we determined that the optimum angle was 70 degrees. We also

The collineal hoe.

determined that a draw hoe of this style cut weeds best when sharpened like a chisel with the sharp edge next to the soil. We now sharpen our hoes by holding them with the handle upright and filing across the upper edge of the blade. I am fascinated by the great improvement in tool performance that can result from such seemingly small refinements. Since the edge of the blade was in line with the handle we called it the "collineal" hoe.

Another tool innovation in our market garden came as a result of changing our transplant system years ago. When we started using soil-block-grown seedlings rather than bare-root plants, we found ourselves holding the transplant trowel in an uncomfortable position. So we made a new tool. We modified a sturdy bricklayer's trowel by shortening the blade and changing the angle of the handle to parallel the blade, thus creating a tool that was comfortable to hold blade-down for jabbing and pulling rather than digging and made a perfect hole for inserting a soil block.

Tool modifications used to be common practice. Many have been forgotten. For example, a newly purchased scythe blade has a standard angle between blade and tang. When scythes were commonly used, everyone understood that it was up to them to bend that angle to fit their mowing style. Another example is that store-bought tools usually come with one length of handle. Is it logical to assume the same handle length will be ideal for tool users from 5'4" to 6'4"? Don't struggle with a handle that is too long or too short—either cut it off or look for a longer one.

The most commonly used tools are easy to find on an outdoor storage wall in summer.

While you are looking at handle length also check out the type of wood and the grain. The preferred woods for tool handles have traditionally been ash for long handles like hoe and shovel and hickory for short handles like axe and maul. The grain can be seen in all those little lines running down the handle. Ideally the lines of grain should run straight from one end of the handle to the other. If the grain lines run at an angle across the handle, the stress of tool use will most likely initiate a break at that point. Once you find a good handle you will want to keep it in shape by coating twice a year with a pure linseed oil or beeswax-linseed mixture. That treatment keeps it from drying out. Dry wood loses its liveliness, becomes brittle, and is more likely to fail.

Often the handle length on old tools had another purpose besides matching the height of the worker. Back when hay was collected loose, long-handled hayforks were used for pitching hay up on to the wagon. A second worker on the wagon used a

shorter fork to make the load stable. Exchange those tools and both workers would have been awkward and inefficient. That long-handled fork was the true "pitch fork." Today pitchfork has become the common name for most tool forks. However, they are functionally very different. Simply learning by name alone that there are hayforks and manure forks and spading forks and garden forks will help you come closer to finding the right tool for the job.

I want to encourage all growers to look beyond the tools that are readily available. Make your farmwork easier and more pleasant by searching out unique tools or creating your own. There are lots of other growers out there looking to pioneer new systems and new crops who can benefit from your ideas and who can in turn inspire you with theirs. We need to invent the future of small farming by ourselves to make all of us more efficient.

# chapter twenty

# Deep-Organic Farming
## and the Small Farm

*First they ignore you. Then they ridicule you.*
*Then they fight you. Then you win.*

—Gandhi

Thor Heyerdahl's classic adventure story *The Ra Expeditions*
has a lesson for agriculture. Heyerdahl wanted to prove that
ancient Egyptian sailors could have reached the New World in
traditional boats made of bundled papyrus stalks. He and his
crew studied fresco paintings, three to four thousand years old,
on tomb walls of pyramids for instruction on how to construct
the crafts. In the paintings there was one rope depicted, extending from the in-curled tip of the stern down to the afterdeck, for
which they could discern no purpose according to modern phys-
ics. In the ensuing construction, it was left out. *Ra I* collapsed
in mid-ocean for lack of that rope. Their second attempt, *Ra II*,
with the newly appreciated rope in its assigned place, completed
the voyage without a hitch.

In the story of agriculture's transition from the natural knowledge of the past to the chemical insults of the present, there was a
part left out that is the rope's equivalent—an unappreciated part
without which the boat will fall apart. That crucial part is called
"soil organic matter." In the mid-1930s, organic farming arose
from a renewed recognition of the vital importance of this soil
ingredient. Some farmers saw the undesirable changes in their
soil and the diminished health of their crops and livestock that
followed the shift to chemical farming in the twentieth century.
Their appreciation for soil organic matter was reborn. They realized that they needed to return to pre-chemical practices, and
improve them where possible, rather than reject them in favor
of chemical shortcuts. They believed this was the direction in
which they needed to go if the health of the soil, the health of
the produce, and the health of the human beings consuming the

produce were to be maintained. Some of their improvements included more successful methods of compost making, symbiotically designed crop rotations, more effective green manuring, better management of plant residues—the leaves, roots, or stems that are left after harvest—and adding mineral nutrients in their most natural form.

The organic pioneers wrote and spoke about their realization that the farm is not a factory, but rather a human-managed microcosm of the natural world. Whether in forest or prairie, soil fertility in the natural world is maintained and renewed by the recycling of all plant and animal residues, which create the organic matter in the soil. This recycling is a biological process, which means that the most important contributors to soil fertility are alive, and they are neither farmers nor fertilizer salesmen. They are the population of living creatures in the soil whose life processes make the plant-food potential of the soil accessible to plants—and their food is organic matter.

The number of these creatures is almost beyond belief. Years ago I was told that a teaspoon of fertile soil contains a million live microscopic organisms. Hard as that may be to believe, the number is now considered far too conservative. Once you begin to understand that the soil is not an inert substance, it's an ecosystem filled with living creatures, a fascinating universe opens in front of your eyes. I once watched a specialist on soil creatures perform a minor miracle. He held the rapt attention of a roomful of teenagers by showing slides and telling tales of the endlessly interrelated and meticulously choreographed activities of these creatures. The students were entranced because the subject matter was like a trip to another planet. They were peeking into the secret world of nature.

The idea of a living soil nourished with organic matter also helps cast light on the difference between a natural and a chemical approach to soil fertility. In the chemical approach, fertilizers created in a factory are applied to the soil to put a limited number of nutrients in a soluble form within reach of plant roots. The chemical idea is to bypass the soil and start feeding the plants directly with preprocessed plant food. In the natural approach, the farmer adds organic matter to nurture all those hard-working soil organisms. The natural approach is usually called *feeding the soil* as opposed to chemically *feeding the plants*, but what it's really doing is feeding the soil creatures. That is why it works so well. The idea that we could ever substitute a few soluble elements for a whole living system is like thinking an intravenous needle could deliver a delicious meal.

## Fighting for the Truth

It is important to stress that what has been accomplished to get organic farming from the early pioneers to where it is today is the story of a groundswell of natural truths flourishing in the face of a passel of corporate/industrial lies. I remember the situation very well as it was when I started back in 1965. The forces were definitely arrayed against us. The defenders of the chemical side, claiming that organic farming was foolish and impossible, were the U.S. Department of Agriculture with its scientists and its enormous budget, all of the land-grant universities and the smaller schools of agriculture, the extension service, every feed and seed store in the country, and of course the enormous money and power of the massive agrochemical industry. On our side, claiming not only that organic farming worked but that it worked much better than chemical farming, were a few old-time large-scale farmers who had never bought into chemicals in the first place and a bunch of idealistic young newcomers who wanted to farm and who found the concepts of organic farming totally in line with their thinking about humanity, sustainability, and the welfare of the planet. When a study came out in 1977 from Barry Commoner's group at Washington University in Saint Louis showing that, in a side-by-side paired comparison, a group of Midwestern organic farmers were just as successful as their chemical-using neighbors, it was the first major eye-opener of the world to come. The other side had had no idea we were that good. There were some newspaper and magazine articles, but far less press than this should have received if the public had been aware of the massively unequal array of

Farmers should always share ideas with each other.

forces on the opposing sides. In my mind what had just happened was the equivalent of a junior high football team splitting a couple of games with the Steelers. The type of press those football games would get is what this incident deserved.

The first of a number of studies positive to organic farming had begun appearing in the early 1970s. I had a friend at the USDA whom I used to call on the phone as each one of these studies appeared. He was consistently dismissive. The first one I told him about was a very positive study by a French farmer's organization. "Ha!" he scoffed, "The USDA isn't going to pay any attention to a bunch of French farmers." A couple of years later a significant study was done by the Dutch Department of Agriculture. "Ha!" he scoffed, "The USDA isn't going to listen to the Dutch Department of Agriculture." Then the

Washington University study came out. "Ha! The USDA isn't going to listen to Washington University." I had lost touch with him by 1980 when the USDA's own very positive study, *Report and Recommendations on Organic Agriculture*, came out, but I would not have been surprised if he had said, "Ha! You don't expect the USDA to pay attention to the USDA, do you?"

And that was, truly, the sad state of affairs. As a fearless early organic farmer, I used to accept all invitations to speak. To be prepared, I did my homework and I spent countless evenings in the stacks of the local university library. I found an enormous number of applicable academic studies published in the major agricultural journals, which reinforced the basic tenets of organic farming. Occasionally, I received invitations from universities themselves. I can remember a number of those speaking engagements. During my talk I would have made a point about soil fertility or plant/pest relationships and there would be an interruption from the audience. "Oh, yes, you're Dean Smith, aren't you?" I would acknowledge the questioner. "Go ahead, what is your question?" "Well, that is the most ridiculous statement I ever heard," he would huff. "Where did that foolishness come from?" I would consult my notes and explain that the information came from recent research published in a major journal and find that the questioner had not read the study.

In other words, the myth that organic farming could not work was so ingrained, so much like a religious belief, that it was accepted out of hand by agricultural-university faculty members who were not reading the published literature in their own fields (or if they were reading, they weren't paying attention). And, of course, none of them had ever investigated it in person. The difficulty of dealing with them reminded me of Max Planck's famous quote: "A new scientific truth does not triumph by convincing its opponents and making them see the light, but rather because its opponents eventually die, and a new generation grows up that is familiar with it."

If the reason for their general disinclination to consider these ideas was that the ideas were brand new, then some of their aversion might be understandable. But they are anything but new. Many

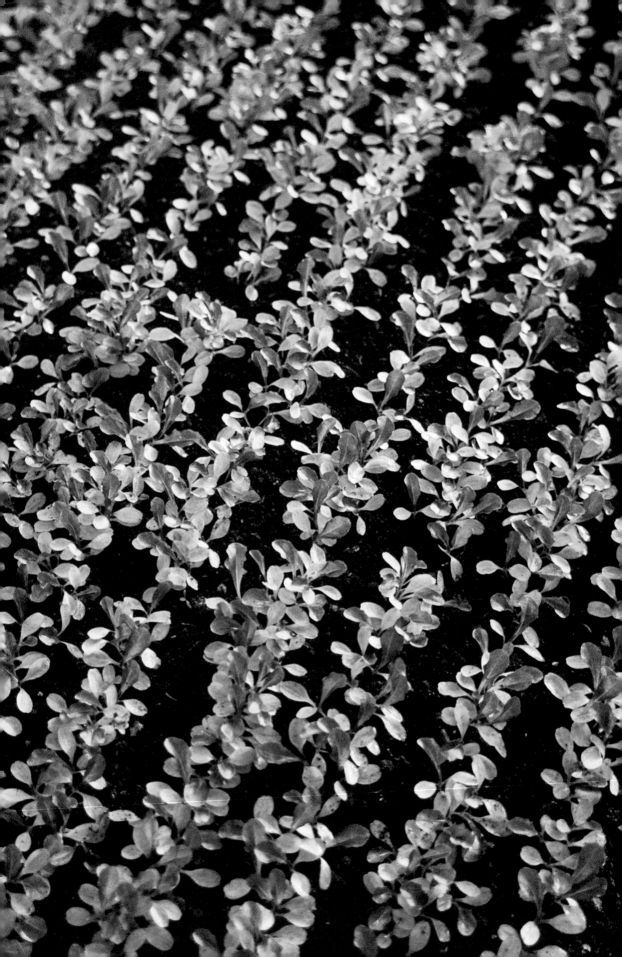

of the books I read when I started out in 1965, books that extolled the benefits of a biological rather than chemical understanding of farming, were already ten years old like P. H. Hainsworth's *Agriculture: A New Approach* (1954), or almost twenty years old like Leonard Wickenden's *Make Friends with Your Land* (1949), or more than thirty years old like Selman Waksman's *The Soil and the Microbe* (1931). Other excellent volumes had been published as much as seventy years earlier. But these ideas were hardly new then. Read K. D. White's tome *Roman Farming* and you will find that the benefits of compost, green manures, mixed farming, crop rotations in general and legume rotations in particular were basic knowledge two thousand years ago. Read F. H. King's *Farmers of Forty Centuries* and you realize they were common knowledge four thousand years ago. Of course they were. How do you think agriculture managed for all those years?

**A perfect bed of young winter lettuce.**

In fact you don't even have to go beyond material published by the USDA itself to be convinced that organic ideas represent sound agricultural thinking. The 1938 Yearbook of the U.S. Department of Agriculture, *Soils and Men*, reads like a basic organic-farming textbook with sentences like these: "While the continuous use of chemical fertilizers tends to deplete the essential elements not supplied to the soil, the use of stable manure, leaf mold, wood ashes and peat tends to conserve them. . . . In some cases soil deficiencies are not revealed by any effect on plant growth, yet the plant is not being supplied with a sufficient quantity of some elements to produce a normal healthy growth of animals feeding on it." And the 1957 Yearbook, *Soil*, is even more emphatic, "Well fed plants usually are less susceptible to soil borne organisms than are poorly nourished plants. Good fertility may so enhance the resistance of the host plant that the parasite cannot successfully attack the roots." "All these experiments point to profound effects of fertilization on the nutritional quality of a plant . . . we will have to determine the balance of plant nutrients in the soil that will produce a plant of optimum nutritional quality."

So how was it in the mid-1960s that organic farming, which concerned itself with exactly the issues raised in those quoted statements, was ridiculed, and chemical farming was called "conventional" agriculture? The farmers didn't do it. Scientists and merchandisers imposed it upon them. Let me tell a metaphorical story from my background. Before I got into farming I was an adventurer. One of my passions was rock climbing. My thinking is still patterned by that rock climbing background. It makes me a problem solver. It makes me adore challenges. Rock climbers, like farmers, are interested in solutions, each one simpler and more elegant than the last. Whereas the rock-cliff scientist, if I may invent such a character, might spend time speculating on the coefficient of friction and surface fracturing between the granitic base and the basalt outcropping or invoking the law of gravity, and the rock-cliff merchandiser might be speculating on what products could be sold to palliate the impossible, the rock climbers would be down at the bottom of the "impossible" cliff quietly studying and planning how to climb it. To the climbers it is a challenge. To the climbers a problem is something to be solved, not something to be studied to death or marketed.

This distinction occurs in part because of the positions from which the different parties see the situation. The scientists and merchandisers are standing far away from the cliff, looking over at it, indulging in their love of reductionism and speculating on the difficulties. The climbers (like farmers) are standing right next to the problem, celebrating their love of solutions and speculating on the possibilities. Where you are looking from and what your goals are determine what you see and what you do. My goals as a farmer are to solve problems, to overcome difficulties, and to do it with my own resources. The goals of the scientists and merchandisers are to study problems, to emphasize the difficulties, and to recommend purchased palliatives.

The implications of this situation are clear. If the cliff can be climbed—and I assure you that it can be—then there are only two options open to the merchandisers and the scientists. First, they can admit that their science and their merchandise are unnecessary because solving the problem has required only imagination and determination. Or, second, they can use all their resources to manipulate the situation through spin and obfuscation so that very few people will know about the climbers and their elegant solution, and the general public will continue to believe it impossible; in other words, to create the climate of ignorance and opposition that organic farming has faced from the start.

The reason for this still very active attempt to villainize organic farming is that our success scares the hell out of the other side. Just like the fear of Nature that the merchandisers and scientists have worked so hard to create in farmers in order to make purchased chemical products and reductionist science seem indispensable, so has our success with organic farming created in the scientists and merchandisers a terrible fear—a fear of their own redundancy; a fear that all farmers will realize other solutions are possible; a fear that agriculture will learn the truth. Organic farmers have succeeded in producing a bounty of food through the simple means of working in harmony with natural processes, without any help from the scientists and the merchandisers. If we rock climbers/farmers can make it up that impossible cliff on our own, then we have proved the commercial interests to be very dispensable indeed, and we are consequently very frightening.

## Who Controls Organic?

Since the 1930s, organic farming has been subjected to the traditional three-step progression that occurs with any new idea directly challenging orthodoxy. First the orthodoxy dismisses it. Then it spends decades contesting its validity. Finally, it moves in to take it over. Now that organic agriculture has become an obvious economic force, industrial agriculture wants to control it. Since the first step in controlling a process is to define (or redefine) it, the U.S. Department of Agriculture hastened to

Salads of cold-hardy colorful baby leaves are a wintertime staple.

influence the setting of organic standards—in part by establishing a legal definition of the word "organic"—and the organic spokespeople naively permitted it.

Wise people had long warned against such a step. Thirty years ago, Lady Eve Balfour, one of the most knowledgeable organic pioneers from the 1930s, said, "I am sure that the techniques of organic farming cannot be imprisoned in a rigid set of rules. They depend essentially on the attitude of the farmer. Without a positive and ecological approach, it is not possible to farm organically." When I heard Lady Eve make that statement at an international conference on organic farming at Sissach, Switzerland, in 1977, the co-option and redefinition of organic by the USDA was far in the future. I knew very well what she meant though, because by that time I had been involved long enough to have absorbed the old-time organic ideas, and I was alert enough to see the changes that were beginning to appear.

When you study the history of almost any new idea it becomes clear how the involvement of the old power structure in the new paradigm tends to move things backwards. Minds mired in an industrial thinking pattern, where farmers are merely sources of raw materials, cannot see beyond the outputs of production. They don't normally consider the *values* of production or the economic benefits to the producers. While co-opting and regulating the organic *method*, the USDA ignored the organic *goal*. But I believe that it is the original organic goal, and not the modern redirection set by the USDA, that can save the family farm, and thus we need to know the difference. To better convey this difference, I like to borrow two words from the ecology movement and refer to "deep" organic farming and "shallow" organic farming.

Deep-organic farmers, in addition to rejecting agricultural chemicals, look for better ways to farm. Inspired by the elegance of Nature's systems, they try to mimic the patterns of the natural world's soil-plant economy. They use freely available natural soil foods from deep-rooting legumes, green manures, and composts to correct the causes of an infertile soil by establishing a vigorous soil life. They acknowledge that the underlying cause of pest problems (insects and diseases) is plant stress; they know they can avoid pest problems by managing soil tilth, nutrient balance, organic-matter content, water drainage, air flow, crop rotations, varietal selection, and other factors to reduce plant stress. In so doing, deep-organic farmers free themselves from the need to purchase fertilizers and pest-control products from the industrial supply network—the mercantile businesses that normally put profits in the pockets of middlemen and put family farms on the auction block. The goal of deep-organic farming is to grow the most nutritious food possible and to respect the primacy of a healthy planet. Needless to say, the industrial agricultural establishment sees this approach as a threat to the status quo since it is not an easy system for outsiders to quantify, to control, or to profit from.

Shallow-organic farmers, on the other hand, after rejecting agricultural chemicals, look for quick-fix inputs. Trapped in a belief that the natural world is inadequate, they end up mimicking the patterns of chemical agriculture. They use bagged or bottled organic fertilizers in order to supply nutrients that temporarily treat the symptoms of an infertile soil. They treat the symptoms of plant stress—insect and disease problems—by arming themselves with the latest natural organic weapons. In so doing, the shallow-organic farmers continue to deliver themselves into the control of an industrial supply network that is only too happy to sell them expen-

A wide selection of the deep organic vegetables we grow on our farm.

sive symptom treatments. The goal of shallow-organic farming is merely to follow the approved guidelines and respect the primacy of international commerce. The industrial agricultural establishment looks on shallow-organic farming as an acceptable variation of chemical agribusiness since it is an easy system for the industry to quantify, to control, and to profit from in the same ways it has done with chemical farming. Shallow-organic farming sustains the dependence of farmers on middlemen and fertilizer suppliers.

The difference in approach is a difference in life views. The shallow view regards the natural world as consisting of mostly inadequate, usually malevolent systems that must be battled or modified. The deep-organic view understands that the natural world consists of elegant, impeccably designed, smooth-functioning systems that must be studied and nurtured. The deep-organic pioneers learned that farming in partnership with the natural processes of soil organisms also makes allowance for the unknowns. The living systems of a truly fertile soil contain all sorts of yet-to-be discovered benefits for plants—and consequently for the livestock and humans who consume them. These are benefits we don't even know how to test for because we are unaware of their mechanism, yet deep-organic farmers are conscious of them every day in the improved vigor of their crops and livestock. This practical experience of farmers is unacceptable to scientists who disparagingly call it mere "anecdotal evidence." Good farmers contend that since most scientists lack familiarity with real organic farming, they are passing judgment on things they know nothing about.

## In Defense of Instinct

It is difficult for organic farmers to defend ideas scientifically where so little scientific data has yet been collected. However, the passion is there because the farmer's instincts are so powerfully sure that differences exist between organic and chemical. I often cite an experience of mine in an unrelated field—music—

in defense of the farmer's instincts. Twice I have been fortunate to hear great artists perform in an intimate setting without the intermediary of a sound system. The first was a sax player, the second a soprano. The experience of hearing their clear, pure tones directly, not missing whatever subtleties a microphone and speakers are incapable of transmitting, was so different and the direct ingestion of the sound by my ears was so *nourishing* (that is the only word I can think of), that I remember the sensation to this day, and use it as a metaphor for differences in food quality. That unfiltered music is like fresh food grown by a local deep-organic grower. That same music heard through a sound system is like industrial organic produce shipped from far away. Through a poor sound system, it is a lot like chemically grown produce.

Like most other farmers, I am aware of the reaction of my customers, especially young customers, as evidence of the advantages of organic over chemical farming. Children are notorious for hating vegetables, but that is not what I hear from parents in the neighboring towns in response to the vegetables we grow on our farm. The eating quality of our vegetables has won out over all the junk-food advertising. We have been told that our carrots are the trading item of choice in local grade-school lunch boxes. Stunned parents have told us that not only will their children eat our salad and eat our spinach; they ask their parents specifically to purchase them. I put great faith in the honest and unspoiled taste buds of children. They can still detect differences that older taste buds may miss and that science cannot measure.

Lately, there has been a lot of talk alerting us to the take-over of many organic labels by the industrial food giants. But to anyone who worries about the survival of small farms, I say the sky is not falling. These takeovers only involve industrial shallow organics. They only involve those companies large enough to attract takeover money. Most of these companies sell processed foods, which are substandard nutritionally, whatever the provenance of their ingredients. When the organic version of the Twinkie eventually appears, it will be immaterial who controls it. Some of these companies do sell staple foods, but they only meet the shallowest of standards, thus ignoring those valuable production practices that only family farmers seem to care about any more.

For example, I don't buy organic eggs from the grocery stores. Merely feeding organic grain to chickens, without giving the animals honest access to the outdoors, does not make a free-range hen or produce truly edible eggs. The yolks of industrial-organic eggs are pale and, being mass-produced somewhere far away, they are not fresh. I purchase eggs from a neighboring farmer who runs her chickens on grass pasture where the sunshine, green food—and a host of unknown factors—result in eggs with deep orange yolks and awesome flavor. I don't buy organic milk from the large producers who keep thousands of cows in confinement and who claim their milk is special because they feed the cows organic grain. As if preventing access to grass is not bad enough, these producers then ultra-pasteurize the cows' milk so they can ship it nationally—thereby destroying the amazing natural cultures and enzymes in uncooked milk. I buy milk from a very successful local raw-milk dairy where the cows eat grass outdoors (as they were designed to do) and produce milk that studies have shown is far richer in many important nutrients due to the grass diet alone.

In other words, the only organic companies that have been bought out are those whose quality is so dubious you don't want to buy their food no matter how many times they can legally print the word organic on the label. Real food comes from local small farms run by deep-organic farmers. These farms won't be bought out because they are too honest and too focused on quality over quantity to attract the takeover specialists. Small, committed, organic family farms are the fastest growing segment in U.S. agriculture today. Old-time deep-organic farming will save these farms because there will always be a demand for exceptional food by astute customers who can see past the hype of the USDA label and realize the importance of making their own fully informed decisions about food quality.

## Asking the Right Questions

In his book *Gravity's Rainbow* Thomas Pynchon says, "If they can get you asking the wrong questions, they don't have to worry about the answers." The question we now need to ask is not "is it organic?" but rather "is it nutritious?" I firmly believe that quality food is vital to the well-being of humans and other animals. Therefore, as a grower, I have an awesome responsibility. Organic farming has to be much more than the absence of the negatives—chemicals and pesticides. The area where organic farming must excel is the presence of the positives—the full nutritional complement of the foodstuff. Scholarly articles by paleopathologists who have studied the skeletal remains of hunter-gatherers remark most significantly on the superior health and stature of the hunter-gatherers compared to modern humans. They attribute the difference to the very natural diet that our ancestors ate. Well, since deep-organic agriculture is a human-managed copy of natural processes, we have it in our power to make our agricultural products as nutritious as those wild foods. We need to make sure we are managing natural processes with the greatest possible skill and care to produce food that contains everything Nature designed it to contain. That means varieties chosen for taste and nutritional value, two factors that are closely related. That means creating growing conditions aimed at optimizing the plants' physiological potential by focusing on quality rather than quantity. The key to that goal is the soil's ability to deliver every mineral in balance. Toward that end, we pay close attention to trace elements, soil aeration, and making exceptional compost.

The success of organic farmers has proven that it is best for the health of the soil not to have our soil food manipulated by industry. Doesn't it follow logically that it is best for the health of humans not to have our human food treated that same way? The food we eat should obviously be fresh, but even more important I want it to be what I call "real." I can't imagine a livestock farmer feeding hay without fiber, silage with preservatives, or ultra-pasteurized milk to a calf, or a grain ration made with white flour, soy margarine, and corn syrup. Dismayingly, prod-

CUKES
BEETS
GREENS
LEEKS
POTATOES
HERBS
FENNEL
ONIONS
TOMATOES
BEANS
CARROTS
CABBAGE
BROCCOLI
CELERY
LETTUCE
SQUASH
ARTICHOKES

FOUR SEASON FARM
FARM STAND

REAL FARMING , REAL FOOD
HOURS
MON~SAT 1PM 5PM CLOSED SUNDAY

The sign at the entrance to our farm is both a marketing tool and a statement of our philosophy.

ucts like that, with "organic" labels, are sold in "health food" stores to be fed to people. That is not my idea of "real food." The vegetables grown on our farm that fill the produce cooler of our local food co-op are real food. But the over-processed products filling the shelves in the rest of the store are not in the same category. One day at lunch when I was ranting about this, I said I wanted to open a store that only sold "real food." My wife, Barbara, who tries to use gentle humor to bring order to my more extreme impulses, said that was nice and since we were talking about "whole" food she had the perfect name for the store: I could call it the "Wholier Than Thou Market."

Well, I am very serious about the need for such a store, although I don't have the time to initiate it myself. I offer the idea and the store name to anyone who would like to take the next step beyond where industrial pressure has stalled the organic movement. This store would sell no prepackaged food. Breads and crackers would be whole grain and made fresh daily. There would be no aged bags of flour but only wheat or oat or rye berries for the customer to grind into fresh flour with the store's mill. Milk would be raw from a local grass-fed herd and so would the butter. If you wanted juices they would be squeezed fresh into your own glass container. Meat, poultry, and eggs would be local and range fed. The fruits and vegetables would be fresh year-round from nearby fields and greenhouses. The only processed foods would be the traditional ones like cheese, yogurt, sauerkraut, pickles, dried tomatoes, wine, and beer. The only sweeteners would be honey and maple syrup. Real food. We all know what it is.

You can easily imagine the displeasure of the organic food processors with the "Wholier Than Thou Market." They are already dismayed at nutritionist Joan Gussow's truthful reference to their products as "value added, nutritionally degraded." But I'm convinced that it is in the best interest of healthy humans to make food processors redundant. Furthermore, all the items in the "Wholier Than Thou Market" would be purchased directly from nearby growers. No middlemen, no energy-intensive long-distance shipping, no need for preservatives. That would make a few other mercenary mercantile groups redundant.

Is this radical? Possibly. But then organic farming seemed pretty radical when I started. Does it make sense? Well, the implications of a large body of nutrition research back it up. Will humans embrace the idea? That depends. The propaganda from the food processors tries to make us think their food is better, just like the propaganda from the chemical companies tried to make us believe their fertilizers were better. Both assertions are false. Eaters and farmers have been sucked in by the intentionally addictive nature of processed foods and processed fertilizers and the relentless advertising behind them. We must now decide that we want to take charge of our body's nourishment as successfully as we have taken charge of our soil's nourishment. Real food, whether for the soil or for the body, takes more time and more commitment. But the reward is the perfect world we would all like to see: happy, healthy human beings optimally nourished with exceptional quality food. The drug companies then become redundant also.

So, how did deep get turned into shallow and good food revert to mediocre? It is a logical result in a world blind to the elegance of natural systems. Humans think in terms of *more* milk rather than *exceptional* milk; *cheaper* eggs not *better* eggs. Since modern humans mistakenly consider nature imperfect, they focus on improving nature rather than seeking to improve our understanding of agriculture and human nutrition within a perfect nature. Humans want to change the rules rather than try to operate more intelligently within them. A recent advertisement from a biotech company pointed that out by highlighting the phrase, "Think what's possible." These companies *think* they have the power to remake the parts of nature they don't understand. However, if they understood them, they would realize they don't need remaking. It is just our human relationship with the natural world that needs remaking.

The historian Howard Zinn has written, "The truth is so often the total reverse of what has been told us by our culture that we cannot turn our heads far enough around to see it." Organic farmers have done an admirable job since the 1930s in turning heads far enough around to see the whole truth about soil nutrition. They have, to return to the Heyerdahl story with which this chapter began, put the rope back in place. It is my hope that the universal year-round availability of fresh, local, "real" food grown by deep organic farmers can allow us to turn heads around far enough to clearly see the whole truth about human nutrition as well.

# Climate Maps

The four climate maps that follow enable comparisons to be made between many factors of the winter climate in different regions of the country:

1. The first map (page 216) shows average January temperatures across the country. It demonstrates that much of the U.S. has the same or warmer January temperatures as does the south of France where winter vegetable production in high tunnels is common practice.

2. The second map (page 217) is the standard USDA zone map. It divides up the country according to minimum temperatures reached during the winter. Our farm in Maine is rated as Zone 5. The zone map is of some use in comparing different parts of the country vis-à-vis how cold it gets, but it does not take into consideration how long the winter goes on.

3. The third map (page 218), titled *Mean Annual Number of Days Minimum Temperature 32°F and Below*, gives a good idea of the length of the winter period. Our farm is located two-thirds of the way up the Maine coast on the 150-day line. A farm in northeastern Missouri with a similar Zone 5 rating from map 2 would be on the 90-day line, quite a difference in length of winter.

4. The fourth map (page 219), *Average Depth of Frost Penetration*, offers another way to look at the severity of the winter. At our location on the coast of Maine the average frost depth is 48 inches. That imaginary farm in northeastern Missouri mentioned above experiences an average frost depth of only 20 inches, quite a difference in severity of winter.

These maps are included in the appendix to help convince growers all across the country to give the winter harvest a try. There are not many places with longer winters than we have here in Maine, but during the 1980s, when I first began seriously experimenting with these ideas, I was living on a farm in the mountains of Vermont in Zone 3. The winter harvest worked just fine there also.

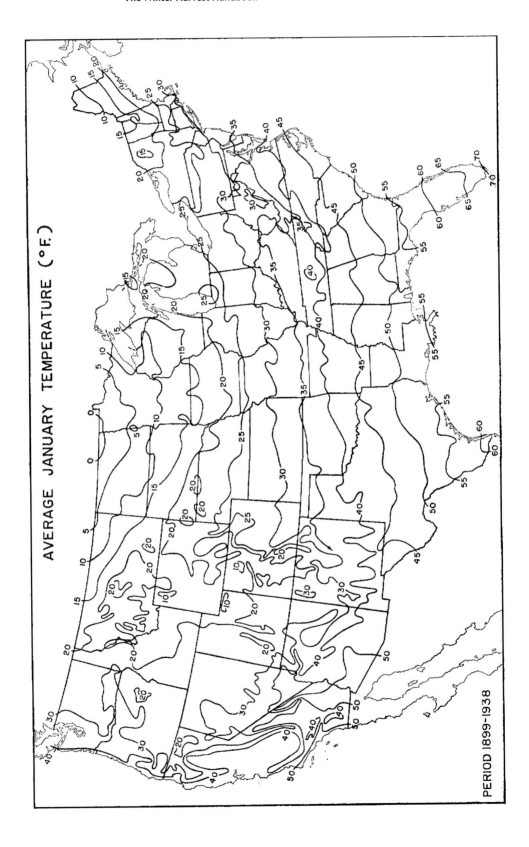

AVERAGE JANUARY TEMPERATURE (°F.)

PERIOD 1899-1938

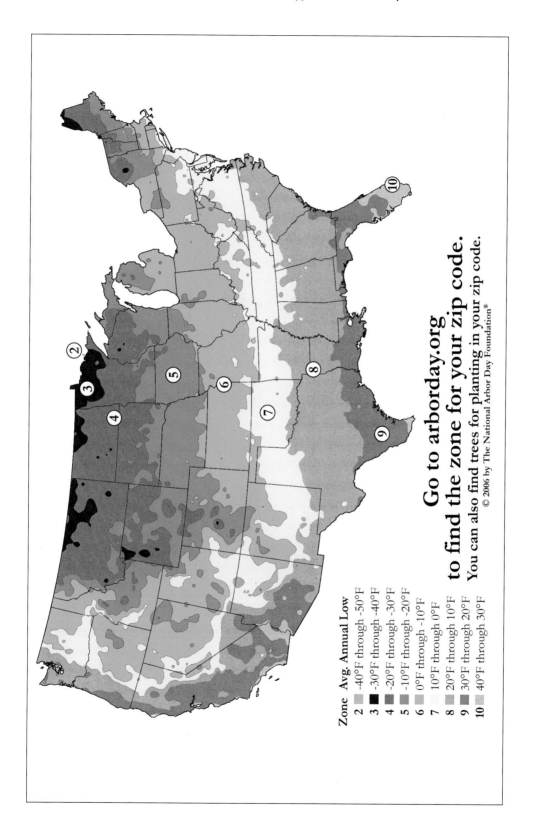

Zone  Avg. Annual Low
2  -40°F through -50°F
3  -30°F through -40°F
4  -20°F through -30°F
5  -10°F through -20°F
6  0°F through -10°F
7  10°F through 0°F
8  20°F through 10°F
9  30°F through 20°F
10  40°F through 30°F

Go to arborday.org
to find the zone for your zip code.
You can also find trees for planting in your zip code.
© 2006 by The National Arbor Day Foundation®

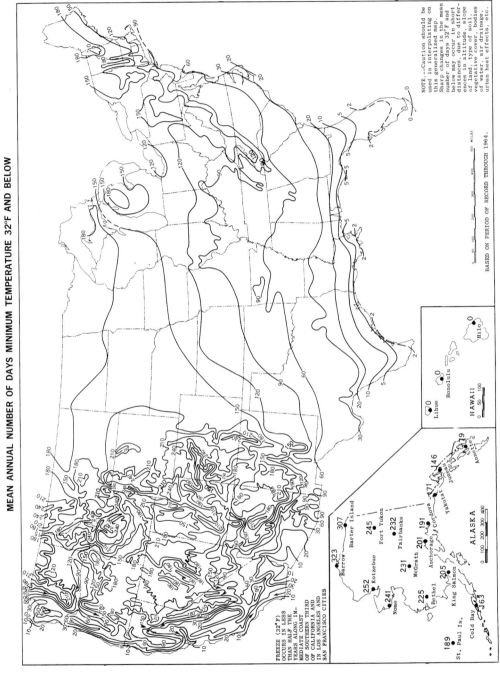

MEAN ANNUAL NUMBER OF DAYS MINIMUM TEMPERATURE 32°F AND BELOW

FREEZE (32°F)
OCCURS IN LESS
THAN HALF THE
YEARS ALONG IM-
MEDIATE COAST
OF SOUTHERN THIRD
OF CALIFORNIA AND
IN LOS ANGELES AND
SAN FRANCISCO CITIES

NOTE.--Caution should be
used in interpolating on
this generalized map.
Sharp changes in the mean
number of days 32°F and
below may occur in short
distances, due to differ-
ences in altitude, slope
of land, type of soil,
vegetative cover, bodies
of water, air drainage,
urban heat effects, etc.

BASED ON PERIOD OF RECORD THROUGH 1964.

ALASKA

Barrow 323
Barter Island 307
Kotzebue 252
Fort Yukon 245
Nome 241
Fairbanks 232
Bethel 225
McGrath 231
Anchorage 201
Cordova 191
King Salmon 205
St. Paul Is. 189
Cold Bay 163
Yakutat 171
Juneau 146
Annette 79

HAWAII
Lihue 0
Honolulu 0
Hilo 0

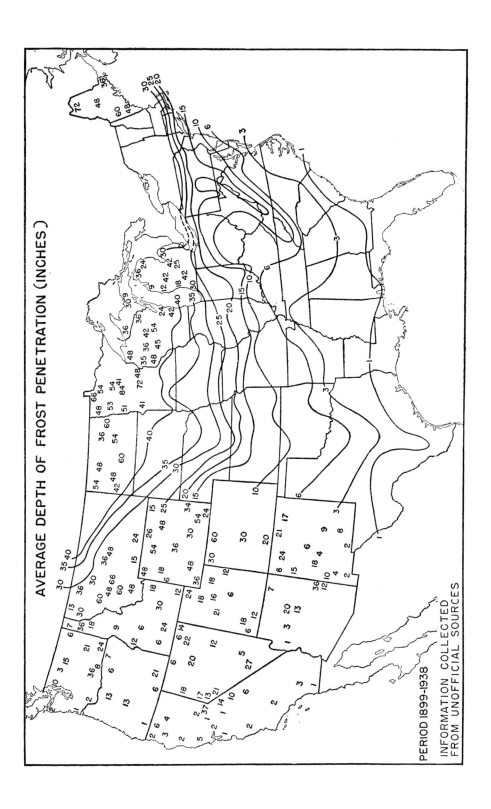

AVERAGE DEPTH OF FROST PENETRATION (INCHES)

PERIOD 1899-1938

INFORMATION COLLECTED
FROM UNOFFICIAL SOURCES

This map and the map on the following page shows how hot the summer gets in different areas of the US. The hotter your summer the better ventilation your greenhouse must have if you wish to grow summer crops. Or you can close the greenhouse during the hottest weeks of summer and solarize the soil. For information, look up "solarizing soil" in your favorite search engine.

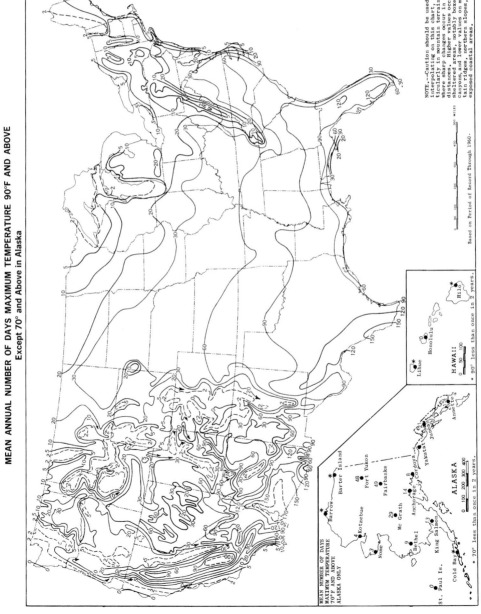

MEAN ANNUAL NUMBER OF DAYS MAXIMUM TEMPERATURE 90°F AND ABOVE
Except 70° and Above in Alaska

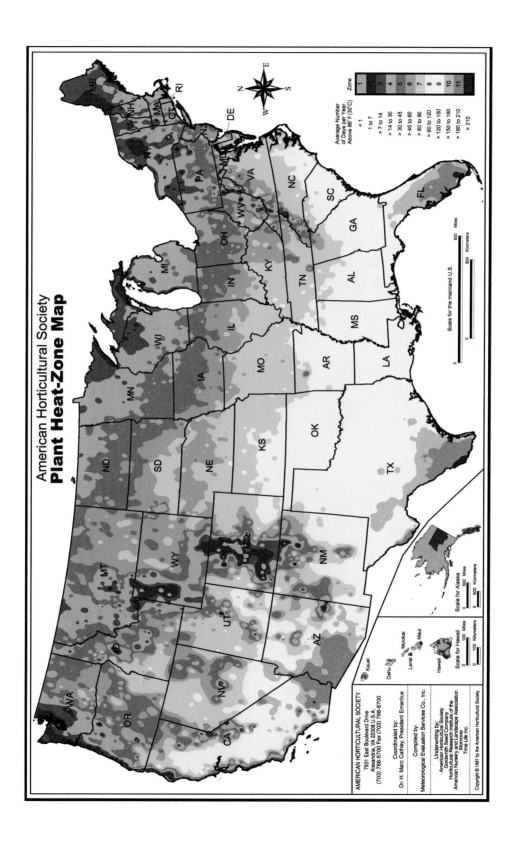

# Effects of Temperature on Plants

120°

115°F – Upper limit. Plants die.

110°

100°

95°F – Maximum photosynthesis. Too hot if continued too long.

90°

80°

75°F – Optimum photosynthesis and plant growth.

70°

60°

55°F – Average daytime greenhouse temperature during coldest months.

50°

40°

35°F – Ideal minimum greenhouse air temperature. No freezing of crops.

30°

20°

15°F – Lower limit for quality harvest of most winter salad crops.

10°

0°

Temperature factors that affect winter salads in protected cultivation:

1. Rate of temperature drop.
2. Depth of temperature drop.
3. Duration of temperature drop.
4. Frequency of temperature drop.

# Tools and Supplies

The six-row seeder, the four-row pinpoint seeder, quick hoops conduit bender for metal conduit, 10-foot-wide row cover and clear plastic for quick hoops, greens harvesters, Victorinox harvest knives, the broadfork, the Tilther, a 30-inch-wide Austrian grading rake, the collineal hoe, the wire weeder, the three-tooth cultivator, the soil block makers, the right-angle trowel, a propane flame weeder, the tomato clips and twine, an excellent European-style scythe (with a folding blade for safe storage), a variety of potting and soil blocking mixes which now includes the entire line of Vermont Compost products, and many other tools are all available from:

Johnny's Selected Seeds
955 Benton Avenue,
Winslow, ME 04901
(877) 564-6697
www.Johnnyseeds.com

The 45-inch-long and 4,000-pound-rated **ground anchors** we use to secure our mobile greenhouses are available from:

A. M. Leonard
PO Box 816
Piqua, OH 45356
(800) 543-8955
www.amleo.com

The best mousetrap to use as a **vole trap** is "The Better Mouse Trap" from Intruder Inc.

230 W. Coleman St.
Rice Lake, WI 54868
(800) 553-5129
www.intruderinc.com

One source of **granular pellets** soaked in predator urine is www. critter-repellent.com. Go to their Web site and click on vole.

Critter-Repellent.Com
PO Box 101
Canisteo, NY 14823
(866) 802-8837

To make our **wire wickets** we purchase 76-inch-long straight lengths of number 9 wire made by Ken-Bar Inc. from our local greenhouse dealer. To locate a dealer for Ken-Bar Inc. in your area contact:

Ken-Bar Inc.
Summit Industrial Park
Peabody, MA  01960
(800) 336-8882
www.ken-bar.com

We purchase **Agribon** row covers for both the greenhouse inner layers and for covering the quick hoops from:

Johnny's Selected Seeds
955 Benton Avenue,
Winslow, ME  04901
(877) 564-6697
www.Johnnyseeds.com

We also have experience with another fabric called **Covertan** Pro 17 from:

Suntex CP, Inc.
PO Box 21633
Sarasota, FL  34276
(888) 786-8391
www.suntexcp.com

We collaborated with Rimol Greenhouse Systems, Inc. in the design and development of a **mobile greenhouse** on wheels. They are selling this greenhouse under the name "Rolling Thunder." Rolling Thunder's design utilizes a heavy-duty wheel with bearings at each set of hoops attached to a specially designed "base post." The wheel/base-post combination is seated on a rail that allows the greenhouse to move along the desired growing areas. Rolling Thunder's design allows for easy movement of a larger greenhouse (such as 30-by-96 feet) with an ordinary tractor. It takes just two individuals to move smaller greenhouses.

When the greenhouse is constructed, the rail is laid out flat according to the desired width of the greenhouse. The rail does not have to be pinned or staked, but should be set on a solid base to prevent sinking into the soil. The first few hoops are the trickiest, requiring several sets of hands due to the fact that the wheels, base posts, and hoops are all erected simultaneously. However, once a few hoops are erected, and diagonally braced, the rest of the greenhouse goes up quickly. There is significant bracing in the greenhouse to prevent any movement with the wind, and temporary bracing is used on the end walls of the greenhouse for stability purposes. The Rimol design allows for flexibility with various height options available through the use of different length base posts.

Rimol Greenhouse Systems
Northpoint Industrial Park
40 Londonderry Turnpike
Hooksett, NH 03106
(603) 629-9004
www.rimolgreenhouses.com

We have also worked with Four Season Tools on the design of their mobile greenhouse that incorporates drop-down side technology on both sides and a full-length roof opening for ventilation. These houses will be available in either wheeled (two options) or sled models. They offer conversion kits to make stationary greenhouses mobile. They are also designing efficient tools for the small farm. Consult their website for the latest developments.

Four Season Tools
602 Westport Road
Kansas City, MO 64111
(816) 444-7330
(816) 561-5052 (fax)
info@fourseasontools.com (e-mail)
www.fourseasontools.com

The pure **cellophane** box liners and bags that we use in our packaging have to be ordered ahead and in sufficient quantity to justify the special sizes. They are available from:

ATLAPAC
2901 East Fourth Ave.
Columbus, OH  43219
(800) 888-7019
www.atlapaccorp.com

## Suppliers

The following seed catalogs offer many varieties suitable for the winter harvest:

**Johnny's Selected Seeds**
955 Benton Avenue,
Winslow, ME 04901
(877) 564-6697
www.Johnnyseeds.com
*Since 1973 supplying a wide range of seeds and tools to fresh market growers and avid home gardeners. Excellent selection of winter harvest varieties.*

**Territorial Seed Company**
PO Box 158
Cottage Grove, OR 97424
(800) 626-0866
www.territorialseed.com
*Publishes a supplementary catalog in June specifically focused on winter gardening.*

**Fedco Seeds**
PO Box 520
Waterville, ME 04703
(207) 873-7333
www.fedcoseeds.com
*Specializes in varieties for northern growers and short growing seasons.*

**Wood Prairie Farm**
49 Kinney Road
Bridgewater, ME 04735
(800) 829-9765
www.woodprairie.com
*Supplier of organic 'Rose Gold' seed potatoes*

**Graines Baumaux**
B.P. 100
54062 Nancy Cedex, FRANCE
Phone 011 33 383 15 86 86
www.graines-baumaux.fr
*The most extensive seed listing of any catalog I know, especially old-time French varieties. You can see their full list at their web site.*

## The Varieties That We Grow

These are the varieties that have worked well for us to date. We have obviously not had the time to run trials on all the cultivars of every crop in every season.

### Winter Crops in the Greenhouse

Asian greens 'Tokyo Bekana', 'Komatsuna', 'Tatsoi', 'Mizuna'
Arugula 'Astro', 'Sylvetta'
Beet 'Red Ace', 'Merlin', 'Touchstone Gold'
Beet leaves 'Bull's Blood', 'Red Ace'
Carrot 'Napoli', 'Mokum', 'Nelson'
Chard 'Fordhook Giant', 'Ruby Red'
Claytonia
Endive 'Bianca Riccia'
Leek 'Tadorna'
Lettuce 'Red Saladbowl', 'Tango', 'Rex', 'Rouge d'hiver'
Mâche 'Vit'
Minutina
Mustard 'Tokyo Beau'
Pak choi 'Mei Qing Choi'
Potato 'Rose Gold'
Radish 'Tinto', 'Cherriette', 'D'Avignon'
Scallion 'White Spear'
Sorrel
Spinach 'Space'
Turnip 'Hakurei'
Watercress

## Summer Crops in the Field and Greenhouse

Artichoke 'Imperial Star'

Basil 'Genovese'

Beans 'Easy Pick'

Broccoli 'Packman', 'Arcadia'

Brussels sprouts 'Oliver', 'Diablo'

Cabbage 'Gonzales', 'Red Express'

Cauliflower 'Fremont', 'Cheddar'

Celeriac 'Diamant'

Celery 'Conquistador', 'Tango'

Corn — *I prefer the simpler old-time varieties because I think they have more real flavor than the super-sweet types.*

Cucumber 'Socrates'

Eggplant 'Orient Express'

Fennel 'Orion'

Garlic — *Whatever variety grows well for you.*

Kale 'Toscano'

Leek 'Upton'

Onion 'Olympic', 'Copra'

Parsley 'Titan'

Parsnip 'Lancer'

Peas 'Strike', 'Lincoln', 'Caseload', 'Maxigolt'

Pepper 'Red Knight'

Potato 'Charlotte'

Radicchio 'Indigo'

Shallot 'French Gray'

Squash 'Butternut'

Tomato 'New Girl', 'Big Beef', 'Tomatoberry Garden'

Zucchini 'Zucchini Elite'

# Sowing Dates for Fall and Winter Harvests

I give only fall dates here because fall is the new planting season for growers to get used to. Once spaces open up following the harvest of these crops, pay attention to crop rotation guidelines and just keep on planting.

These fall-planting dates are specific to our location and climate. I include them to offer others a frame of reference for determining their own dates. We are not entirely satisfied with the precision of these dates yet and will be adding more dates as we fine-tune our production in the years to come. No dates are given for crops where we are not sure of our recommendations. The best advice is to sow often and keep notes.

We plant in four different sites for fall and winter harvesting: (1) the outdoor fields where we harvest until early November; (2) the early greenhouses; (3) the later greenhouses; and (4) the cool greenhouse. Dates in **bold** indicate sowings planned for multiple harvests.

| Crop | Outdoor | Early House | Late House | Cool House |
|------|---------|-------------|------------|------------|
| Arugula | 9/4, 9/8, 9/12, 9/16 | 9/22, 9/24, 9/26, 9/28, 9/30, 10/2 | | 10/20, 10/25, 10/30, **11/4, 11/15, 12/10** |
| Beet Leaves | **8/26, 8/30** | **9/2, 9/6** | 9/10 | 10/1, 10/5 |
| Carrot | 7/25, 8/1 | 8/3, 8/7 | | 11/30 |
| Claytonia | **8/20** | **9/2** | 9/18, 9/27 | |
| Endive | 8/10, 8/16 | 8/20 | | **10/6, 10/12, 10/16, 11/5** |
| Lettuce | 8/29, 9/2 9/4, 9/6 | 9/13, 9/15 9/17 | **9/19, 9/22, 9/25, 9/28** | 10/24, 10/30 **11/5, 11/8, 11/11** |
| Mâche | | | 9/24, 9/28, 10/2, 10/6, 10/9, 10/12 | |
| Minutina | 8/20, 8/25 | 9/2 | **9/18, 9/26** | 10/10, 10/15, 10/20 |
| Spinach | **8/22 – 9/3** | **9/5 – 9/8** | **9/12, 9/18, 9/21, 9/24** | |
| Turnip | 8/20, 8/26, 9/1, 9/4, 9/7, 9/9 | 9/20, 9/24 | | 10/10, 10/14, 10/17, 10/20 |

## Historical Reading List

Aquatias, P. *Intensive Culture of Vegetables on the French System*. London: L. Upcott Gill, 1913. This book states that "manure, water, and labor . . . constitute the backbone of intensive culture" and describes how to apply those three in the successful production of year-round vegetables.

Bailey, L. H. *The Forcing Book*. New York: The Macmillan Company, 1897. Complete and carefully presented, this is a classic Liberty Hyde Bailey book. The bulk of his information is just as valuable today as it was back then.

Dreer, Henry A. *Dreer's Vegetables Under Glass*. Philadelphia: Henry A. Dreer, 1896. Dreer was obviously skilled at his craft. In addition he had done enough traveling to comment knowledgeably on the techniques of other growers. He has an easy writing style and provides clear and concise information. This little book is a real gem.

Henderson, Peter. *Gardening for Profit*. New York: Orange Judd Company, 1907. This is the classic of classics. First published in 1867, it was the first American book devoted to market gardening, and it inspired a host of people to give it a try. Still a great source of information all these years later.

Kropotkin, Peter. *Fields, Factories and Workshops*. New York: G. P. Putnam's Sons, 1901. Kropotkin was a perceptive observer of the agricultural realities of his time. This small volume has been referred to in *The Ecologist* as "one of the canonical texts of the ecological tradition."

Macself, A. J. *French Intensive Gardening*. London: W. H. & L. Collingridge Ltd., 1932. This is good hard data from a competent practitioner. Excellent drawings and photos are included to clearly illustrate every aspect of the craft.

McKay, C. D. *The French Garden in England*. London: The Daily Mail, 1909. One of the early small books that attempted to popularize the practices of the French growers.

It's nice to see such passion for the idea that small-scale food production can be a successful profession.

Newsome, T. *Gold Producing Soil*. Stroud: Frederick Steel & Co., 1908. This is a very enthusiastic and reasonably complete presentation of the French system.

Nussey, Helen, and Olive Cockerell. *A French Garden in England*. London: Stead's Publishing House, 1909. A record of the successes and failures of a first year of intensive culture by two young women graduates of Lady Warwick's Gardening School. A realistic account by two beginners.

Robinson, William. *The Parks and Gardens of Paris*. London: John Murray, 1883. You can read this wonderful old book online thanks to Google's digital library project.

Smith, Thomas. *French Gardening*. London: Joseph Fels, 1909.

————. *The Profitable Culture of Vegetables*. London: Longmans, Green and Co., 1919.

The wealthy American soap manufacturer Joseph Fels, who had been involved with providing gardens for workers in Philadelphia, bought land in England to help small-scale intensive vegetable producers get established. Thomas Smith was his farm manager. These books give a clear presentation of the successful production systems they used.

Weathers, John. *French Market-Gardening*. London: John Murray, 1909. Not as complete as some of the others but still worth reading because of Weathers' extensive experience. The introduction is by William Robinson, who first brought the successes of the French growers to the attention of the English.

## Winter-Harvest Reading List

Anonymous. *Blocks for Transplants*. Grower Guide No. 10. London: Grower Books, 1980.

———. *Cucumbers*. Grower Guide No. 15. London: Grower Books, 1983.

———. *Lettuce Under Glass*. Grower Guide No. 21. London: Grower Books, 1981.

———. *Peppers and Aubergines*. Grower Guide No. 3. London: Grower Books, 1986.

———. *Vegetables Under Glass*. Grower Guide No. 26. London: Grower Books, 1982.

The above books were written for chemical growers using mostly heated greenhouses, but the basic information is system-neutral and very complete. Grower Books, a branch of England's leading grower's magazine, used to publish a number of small volumes like these on a wide range of vegetable topics.

Artiss, Percy. *Market Gardening*. London: W. H. & L. Collingridge Limited, 1948. A little-known book by a competent grower who was almost organic without saying so. "The soil must be biologically healthy." He gives very thorough coverage of every aspect of field and greenhouse cultivation.

Coleman, Eliot. *The New Organic Grower*. Revised edition. White River Junction, VT: Chelsea Green, 1995. *The New Organic Grower* provides indispensable background information on soil-fertility management and cultural techniques for both field and greenhouse vegetable growers. The information in *The Winter Harvest Handbook* complements and updates the winter-harvest chapters in this earlier book.

Gerst, Jean-Jacques. *Legumes sous baches*. Paris: Centre Technique Interprofessionel des Fruit et Legumes (CTIFL), 1993. The title translates as "Vegetables Under Covers." This is a technical manual for French growers. It is professional and practical. The contents include every possible vegetable and every imaginable combination of high tunnels, low tunnels, reflective covers, floating covers, and heated and unheated greenhouses. The book is written for more temperate climates than mine, but that doesn't make it any less valuable. If you don't speak French it is worth learning the language or marrying a French speaker just so you can read this book.

Larcom, Joy. *Oriental Vegetables*. New York: Kodansha International, 1991. This is the volume we consulted when we began to explore the vast trove of potential Asian crops. Everything you ever wanted to know and more.

Lawrence, William J. C. *Science and the Glasshouse*. Edinburgh: Oliver and Boyd, 1948. Lawrence is my favorite old-time greenhouse writer because he was so tireless in trying to pin down what did work, what didn't, and why. His experiments are fun to read about and his conclusions are of great practical value. An earlier book of his, *Seed and Potting Composts* (1939), was my indispensable guide when I was trying to formulate my own potting mixes.

Nisley, Charles H. *Starting Early Vegetable and Flowering Plants Under Glass*. New York: Orange Judd, 1929. This is a very professional book with information on plants, horticultural techniques, and building glasshouses and frames. There are lots of black-and-white photos of the field and greenhouse vegetable industry in the 1920s.

Van den Muijzenberg, Edwin W. B. *A History of Greenhouses*. Wageningen, Netherlands: Privately published, 1980. The story of greenhouse development from the earliest recorded examples up through modern Dutch glasshouses makes for fascinating reading.

Wittwer, S. H., and S. Honma. *Greenhouse Tomatoes, Lettuce, and Cucumbers*. East Lansing: Michigan State University Press, 1979. Although some of the material is dated, this is still a good book to introduce beginners to the techniques involved.

# Index

# About the Author

Eliot Coleman has nearly 40 years of experience in all aspects of organic farming, including field vegetables, greenhouse vegetables, rotational grazing of cattle and sheep, and range poultry. He is the author of *The New Organic Grower* and *Four-Season Harvest*. He has contributed chapters to three scientific books on organic agriculture and has written extensively on the subject since 1975. He also wrote the foreword to *Preserving Food Without Freezing or Canning*, by the gardeners and farmers of Terre Vivant.

During his careers as a commercial market gardener, the director of agricultural research projects, and as a teacher and lecturer on organic gardening, he has studied, practiced, and perfected his craft. He served for two years as the Executive Director of the International Federation of Organic Agriculture Movements and was an advisor to the US Department of Agriculture during their landmark 1979-80 study, *Report and Recommendations on Organic Farming*.

He has conducted study tours of organic farms, market gardens, orchards, and vineyards in Europe and has successfully combined European ideas with his own to develop and popularize a complete system of tools and equipment for organic vegetable growers. He shares that expertise through his lectures and writings, and has served as a tool consultant to a number of companies. He presently consults and designs tools for Johnny's Selected Seeds.

With his wife, Barbara Damrosch, he was the host of the TV series *Gardening Naturally* on The Learning Channel. He and Barbara presently operate a commercial year-round market garden, in addition to horticultural research projects, at Four Season Farm in Harborside, Maine.

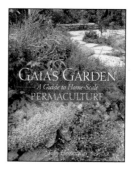

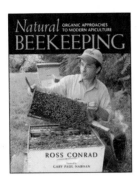

*Natural Beekeeping*
*Organic Approaches to Modern Apiculture*
ROSS CONRAD
ISBN 978-1-933392-08-0
Paperback • $35.00

*The Flower Farmer*
*An Organic Grower's Guide to Raising*
*and Selling Cut Flowers*
Revised and Expanded
LYNN BYCZYNSKI
ISBN 978-1-933392-65-3
Paperback • $35.00

*Sharing the Harvest*
*A Citizen's Guide to Community*
*Supported Agriculture*
Revised and Expanded
ELIZABETH HENDERSON with ROBYN VAN EN
ISBN 978-1-933392-10-3
Paperback • $35.00

*Renewing America's Food Traditions*
*Saving and Savoring the*
*Continent's Most Endangered Foods*
Edited by GARY PAUL NABHAN
ISBN 978-1-933392-89-9
Paperback • $35.00

CHELSEA
GREEN
PUBLISHING

the politics and practice of sustainable living

For more information or to request a catalog,
visit **www.chelseagreen.com** or
call toll-free **(800) 639-4099**.